LIFE after LOSS

GW00775705

LIFE after LOSS

Getting over Grief
Getting on with Life

FRANCIS MACNAB

MILLENNIUM BOOKS

First published 1989 by
Millennium Books Pty Ltd
3/32-72 Alice Street, Newtown
NSW 2042 Australia
Reprinted 1993
© Francis Macnab 1989

National Library of Australia, Cataloguing-in-Publication data
Macnab, Francis.
   Life after loss.

   Bibliography.
   ISBN 0 85574 879 6.

   1. Bereavement — Psychological aspects. 2. Grief.
   3. Loss (Psychology). 4. Adjustment (Psychology).
   I. Title.

155.9'3

Library of Congress, Cataloging-in-Publication data
Macnab, Francis.
   Life after loss : getting over grief, getting on with life /
   Francis Macnab.
        p.   cm.
   Bibliography: p.
   ISBN 0-85574-888-5 : $17.95 — ISBN 0-85574-879-6 (pbk.)
   1. Grief. 2. Bereavement—Psychological aspects.
   3. Loss (Psychology). I. Title.
BF575.G7M33 1989   89-8267
155.9'37—dc20   CIP
Edited by Lynn Gemmell
Text designed by Helen Semmler, Cover designed by Liz Vogdes
Typeset in 12/14 Goudy by Thomas Marsden Advertising Pty Ltd
Printed in Australia by Australian Print Group, Maryborough

Contents

I know the paths of the soul, overgrown, often know only the night, a very vast, very barren night, without landscapes. And yet I tell you: we'll get out. The most glorious works of man are born of that night.

Elie Wiesel

Introduction

That which does not kill me makes me stronger.

Friedrich Nietzsche

At a critical time in my life I stood on the bridge at Banchory not far from Aberdeen in Scotland. The River Feugh at this spot is a fast-rushing stream, and as it gushes and cascades over huge layers of rocks and through the profusion of crevices, there is a massive turbulence of froth and water.

When it would have been simpler for the salmon to defy their inbuilt call of nature and stay downstream, they did the opposite. Against the rush of the current they made their leap upstream. Against what seemed like impossible odds: layers and ledges of rock, cracks and crevices, they leapt and fell, lay steady as if gathering new resources, then made their further leap.

Upstream and far beyond the rocks, the salmon would arrive. Their arduous journey was ended, and a new generation, another life cycle, was about to begin.

John Ormond in his poem *Salmon* wrote thus:

... A hundred times
They lunge and strike
Against the hurdles of the rock;
Though hammering water
Beats them back
Still their desire does not break.
They coil and whip and kick,
Tensile for their truth's
Sake; give to the miracle
Of their treadmill leaping
The illusion of the natural ...

Sometimes the human being when dealing with the stresses of life stays downstream and drifts onward into the ocean. At other times the human being can be like the salmon. As if responding to some greater call of nature he will turn upstream and, negotiating a course through stressful events and difficult odds, will continue to leap. Drawn toward a destination upstream, the human being there fulfills one part of destiny and there also begins another.

Although the pathway and achievements of the salmon are for human beings both satisfying and inspiring, the realities are frequently difficult and painful. We are particularly concerned here with the stresses of loss and grief and how we might get beyond the pains of these stresses and if possible be broadened and strengthened in the process.

Loss and grief are associated most acutely with the death of a significant person. But many other events and experiences bring the pain of loss and grief. Some will recount how a death experience was easier to manage than the traumas of rejection, separation and divorce; or the pain of loneliness, of homesickness or of being a refugee or a migrant separated from family, known places and a language that could be understood. Some go through intense disruption and anxiety as they pass through the transitions of life, as they realize they are aging or as they try to adapt to retirement after years of a high-status active involvement in work or various organizations. Others feel deeply the loss of strongly held hopes and expectations, the discovery of flaws in valued relationships or the awareness that they are vulnerable to the invasion of distressing memories, anxieties about the future and the perception of the rapidity of change.

Some of these stresses are imposed from without, some are necessary and expected parts of the normal human life cycle and some become powerful hindrances to growth and happiness because of the inner stresses we create about them and the many further problems we associate with them.

Loss and grief can be painful experiences. We all know about physical pain. We want to get rid of it as quickly as possible. Our emotional pain is more constantly with us. It can affect us more comprehensively and deeply, and it has far-reaching repercussions long after the pain is past. Yet we are often confused about our emotional pain and its management. How do we get over it? Do we ever get over it? With physical pain, we can say, "It is over." We may not have a clear memory of what it was like after it has gone, and we would have difficulty reinvoking it. But with emotional pain, one glimpse of a photograph, one word, a stray thought, can throw us into a worse emotional state than when the trauma first occurred. Emotional pain may occur with or without direct contact with the trauma. It can occur by imagination or empathy and by the telling of a story. Later, the memory of the story may be sufficient to evoke a strong and sustained reaction in the listener and in those close to the listener.

There are times when we can experience some satisfaction and exhilaration from this, as we enter into the emotions of a play, an opera or music.

In this book, I am concerned to set out ways whereby we can find the quickest possible relief from the emotional pain of our loss and grief. There is nothing especially sacred about this type of pain that it should be sustained; we need to get over it and get on with life. Some have focused attention on the processes associated with grief and bereavement. Others have followed the ways people have carried their grief and worked at its various associated manifestations, and they have plotted stages and pathways of grief and loss. The processes of so-called grief work and mourning have been based on observations and reports of bereaved people, and not infrequently out of a great deal of sentimental identification with them.

This book is a major departure from such an approach. It clearly states the goal of recovery and relief within the shortest possible time span. It gathers together our knowledge and experience of coping psychology and the management of post-traumatic stress disorders, and sets out some directions and zones of concern for helping people reach these stated goals. Here we are not only evolving attitudes toward grief based on grieving experiences but this book presents a framework and a body of knowledge and procedures for grieving people to get free of their pain.

Our former approaches to the management of loss and grief have perhaps unwittingly followed the biological model which concentrated on the blocking and flowing of energy. There is no doubt that in grief, and in its many associated ailments, physical and emotional energy is involved. We get a far more embracive picture, however, when we see how much our information systems are involved, from the moment we register the loss to how it is interpreted emotionally, interpersonally, physically, spiritually, unconsciously and neurologically. The information approach at once involves the sufferers in personal participation and personal responsibility for their health and well-being.

Rather than seeing loss as something which has been inflicted and which has to be endured, the focus is turned to the distressed persons, for them to become responsive and active partners in the process of their own rehabilitation and new beginning.

With former approaches, it was common to accept that people were passive victims of their traumas and losses, and their reactions. It was acceptable to proffer like an oracle that "there were certain pains that people never get over." We know, however, that people facing identical traumas will show a wide variety of response to them. It is possible by an information approach to encourage people to change attitudes and their ways of thinking and behavior to help them to a more constructive coping with the traumas and their inner reactions. People have an important part to play in being responsive to what impinges upon them, and to how they perceive the events of life, themselves and the nature of things in the context of their world view and general philosophy of life.

My view expressed in this book is that emotional pain — like any other pain — should be subjected to strategies of relief and rehabilitation as an early priority and goal. To do this it is important to listen to the language of grief experiences, so that relief can be appropriate and specific to the pecular pains that are being described.

With loss we are at once confronted by a new reality. It may be both unexpected and unwanted and many strategies may be used to avoid it. But each of us has to face that new reality and address it, not as a totally negative destiny, but as a challenge to be shaped and constructively organized.

The process involves new ways of thinking about the stress, ourselves, our resources and life itself. Inevitably memory, imagination and ruminations of the mind keep trapping us back into morbid preoccupations and non-coping. We can develop ways of reorganizing the inner-mind ruminations and of relieving distressing memories. The mind often runs out of control; we worry irrationally and become anxious and distressed to a point where daily functioning is impaired and our self-confidence is at a low ebb. We set out here how it is possible to retrain the mind in its focus and restore self-confidence and self-esteem.

People who are entangled by the experiences of loss and grief begin to adopt behavior that reflects their experience, and that also sustains and reinvokes that experience. We can intercept that behavior and begin to practice behavior that will reflect coping behavior and will work to counter the erosive forces of those losses and our inner dialogue and attitudes about them.

Whenever we experience severe loss, our life-style is likely to be affected. Life-styles are not only individual experiences; they are developed and endorsed by society. Our losses affect both individual life-styles and our cultural life-styles. Better coping will involve reshaping these life-styles.

As religion traditionally has been part of the management of losses (particularly those associated with death) this book provides a review of some religious thinking. This leads to a reconsideration of what a funeral can be in the context of a responsive individual and community re-evaluation.

Loss and grief reactions necessarily involve our bonds of love and attachment and the way these bonds are broken and re-formed. This book concludes with comments on our loving and the way we might prepare ourselves for our losses and for the enhancement of life through ongoing and different experiences of love.

Thus, in summary, this book sets out these zones for deliberation and action:

1 Experiences of grief
2 The language of grief
3 Painful feelings and the goal of rehabilitation
4 The new reality
5 Ways of thinking
6 Ruminations of the mind
7 Focusing of the mind
8 Sorting out our body reactions
9 How we will behave
10 Life-style and the future
11 The place of religion
12 The final observances
13 The bonds of love and the way we love
14 A better management.

Whereas some of our losses hardly affect us (we take them in our stride and integrate them within our life history and experience) other losses can have long and painful effects. A teacher made an error in disciplining a child in his first appointment to a school. He later discovered that he had disciplined the wrong child. Within the context of experiences, that child became mentally disturbed and spent some years in a hospital. The teacher believed he had caused the mental illness; he lost his belief in himself as a teacher and grieved over his error and the hurt he believed he had inflicted. This pain accompanied him throughout his career and affected his decisions, his relationships and his behavior.

A young doctor in his early years of practice wrongly diagnosed the illness of a young woman. She died. The pain of his error affected him until long after he retired. He felt that in that faulty diagnosis he had lost his capacity and right to be a doctor, and though he withdrew into laboratories, isolating himself from direct patient contact, he continued to feel that by not surrendering his license to practice, he had lost his integrity and eventually life would catch up with him. It seemed to do so in the various illnesses and ailments from which he suffered through his lifetime and through a recurring depression that made him an unhappy person both in his home and at work.

In the past we have focused a great deal of attention on the nature of the trauma, and often made strong speculations about its inevitable and long-term effects on the victim or the sufferer, without adequate awareness and recognition of the factors which can play a critical part in the person's reaction and well-being. We have been understandably concerned about the individual person's reaction to the trauma and have made a direct causal link between that reaction and the trauma, without always paying heed to other factors which may be part of the reaction and sustaining it.

Grief is by no means a single reaction. There are many griefs. They all come within the context of post-traumatic stress symptoms and disorders. We have come to see that the post-traumatic symptom is not simply and causally related to the trauma. Symptom relief will be affected by:

1   The person's attributes before the trauma occurred:

their self-esteem and self-worth, their inner strengths, their attitudes, values and philosophy of life

2 The person's past history: their past experience of stress, their developmental experiences, their models, their general attunement to life

3 The way the person perceives the trauma, evaluates its significance and appraises their own capacity to cope with it

4 The disruption and amount of stress created by the trauma, the areas of life affected, the repertoire of resources available

5 The social context at the time of the trauma and afterwards, the support available, the significant relationships and how they are perceived, experienced and used

6 The repertoire of coping resources and strategies that are available and that can be put into action, attitudes to deal with life's problems and the capacity to sustain a positive sense of emotional wellbeing

7 The ongoing and changing social environments which help the person get over their pain or which, in various overt and subtle ways, tend to provide the climate for recurring symptoms

8 The role of imagination, thought processes and conscious and unconscious wishes that affect the course of symptoms; which help to release the person or turn them toward regressive thinking and behaviour

9 The memory of the events, the meaning of the memories and the symbolic and metaphoric significance they come to have for the person's life

10 The readiness of society to change.

The emphasis on the person's pain may overlook that some important human problems are not responsive to individual human efforts. Better coping, well-being and health depend also on the responsiveness, intervention and change in society itself, in its attitudes, rituals and behavior.

Psychology and clinical practice have now gathered together a body of knowledge and experience which can move us toward a more effective way of coping with loss and grief.

The emotional pain of grief takes its toll on people's health and morale, their feeling and functioning, their enjoyment of life and sense of well-being. It is frequently accompanied by yearning and fretting, tearfulness and emptiness, physical sensations, illness and nausea. As with some states of depression grief may bring loss of interest in the world or it may drive people obsessively. It may be accompanied by loss of appetite or voracious eating, by slowing down of activities or agitation, by sleep disturbances or long periods of tiredness or deep sleep. There may be anguish and remorse, guilt and self-criticism, wishful and magical thinking.

"If only it had not happened."

"It should not have happened like this."

"What if ..."

"What if I had been a second sooner ..."

"What if he had not done that ..."

Emotionally, grieving people may be sad or enraged, sullen and withdrawn or aggressive and demanding. They may benefit from every offer of help or they may be inconsolable. Spiritually, they may question the meaning and purpose of life; they may resent the injustice and unfairness of it all; they may target themselves as being singled out to suffer. They may question the sense of believing in God or following a religion, or they may go overboard in their beliefs about an afterlife and their ability to communicate with the dead person.

We take cognizance of the extent of the anguish and pain associated with loss and grief. The pain and restlessness can be so distressing that grieving people turn desperately to other relationships, search for any solution, turn to various chemical aids and comforts. Sometimes these are necessary and helpful; at other times they create additional problems and new conditions in the body or the family. They become what is known as iatrogenic problems (caused by the treatment) and they themselves may require treatment.

People react to losses in vastly different ways. There are no fixed, prescribed or predicted ways or stages. There are some who have no experiences of loss that they would describe as significant, yet cope successfully when faced with a catastrophe of losing a house and all its contents in a flood.

One woman said, "I never imagined anything like that ever happening to me. I had never experienced any loss, no one close to me has ever died. I have been so fortunate. In fact, it was the awareness that I had been so fortunate that seemed to give me strength to cope. I looked at my children who were all looking miserable and said, 'Come on kids! It's only a house.' And we all laughed, and went over to the fellow who was making arrangements for some campers to be brought in."

This woman's readiness to begin coping and her belief that she would cope took precedence over a preoccupation with the loss of the house and all their belongings. We see how her attitude and the flow of information gave perspective to the disaster and to the necessary problem-solving.

Another woman had been through five years of the Lebanon war. She had been bombed out of two homes; her parents and two of her brothers had been killed in the war. She had seen many people maimed and killed. She was astonished that she and her husband and two teenage sons were able to escape and build a new home in Australia. One of the sons committed suicide at the age of 18. She was devastated. For months she was depressed and wanting to die. Nothing consoled her. She remained preoccupied with the loss and was overwhelmed by her reaction to it. Despite earlier encounters with tragedy and loss in a war environment she was astonished to find she was so incapacitated by her son's death. A pathway marked by earlier experiences of loss did not in itself mean that a loss with a specific meaning would be the easier to manage.

To the same stress, one member of the family may react with great pain and distress, another with relief, even elation. Many react in ways that follow custom and convention; others are uncertain about how to react — they imitate others, behave in ways that reflect the books they have read, or add to the chaos that has befallen them. There are people who recover quickly from their trauma and loss; others are much slower. There are those who have been through extensive and multiple tragedies and have returned to the full flow of life, with very little apparent need to return to or remain in their grief. Others with seemingly "easier" losses become entangled in their reactions and ruminations that persist for years.

I have seen victims of large-scale disasters, ex-prisoners of war, survivors of the Holocaust and children of the survivors. For some, their memories are vivid and their restlessness acuminated; for others, their current situation — what they are doing and how they perceive themselves

— seems more important. The memories recede, fragment or become integrated as events of their biography. On the other hand, I have seen how a person can be drawn into an organization, or a new social context, which can arouse and provide the cause for recurring post-traumatic symptoms and distress.

Our task is to find effective ways to get over those emotional pains — to let them go — and grow despite the inducements to hold onto them. On the one hand we recognize the need to get over the pain, but on the other hand it clings to us — or we to it. Clinging to it can be a way, an unsatisfactory way, of maintaining some link with the person or the event which has been lost. It can be our way of continuing our guilt and punishment and the debt we have come to believe we owe the one who has gone. It can also be our way of accepting ourselves as living an impaired existence. The pain becomes a metaphorical expression of what life generally, and our life in particular, has become.

We need to take careful notice of the fact that many people cling to their pain because they do not know how to let it go, and they have never learned. They have never thought through their philosophy or the assumptions that underlie their behavior. Others have no model to follow, or the models they have are the models of pain, where a parent, perhaps, also bore unnecessary suffering as a way of being in mourning or a way of demonstrating that they did not and should not get over their loss and grief. Clinging to grief and pain can become a deceptive way of protecting ourselves from life and growth, as we adopt the role and mode of being a bereaved person.

Other impediments to relinquishing and relieving our emotional pain are readily available. Ideology and dogma gather around our traumas and interfere with the application of effective coping strategies and question their legitimacy. I heard one distinguished doctor say, "You never get over a child-death. That's the worst death of all." I knew that was not a universal truth even though it was stated as if it were. It was not long before I discovered that the doctor herself had experienced the death of a child. A kind of exclusive elitism had surrounded her: "If you haven't been through such an experience, how would you ever know what it was like?" She built a strong reputation around this dogma which itself is part of a wider dogma that there are different kinds of death. The dogma confuses the observation that people do indeed die in different ways with the metaphor that death after it has occurred is somehow different for one person from what it is for another. It also confuses the event of the death with the way it is perceived, with the appraisal of a particular person in a particular context and time.

Alongside the dogma that a baby-death is the "worst death" we could consider the experience of four children aged 8, 12, 15 and 16, who were brought to see me by their father. A month earlier the father and mother were taking their dog for a walk in the park on a quiet autumn evening. The husband, who had the dog on a leash, stopped while the dog did its sniffing. An assailant sprang on his wife, inflicted heavy blows to her head, snatched her bag and fled. The woman was admitted to hospital with a broken jaw and brain damage. She died two days later. What of the husband's grief and that of the children? Would these children experience this as a less significant death, and loss, than the doctor would experience the loss of her infant? These traumatic reactions do not yield to generalizations and dogmas, but depend on the perception and resources of the individuals concerned, on the bond that existed and was perceived to exist prior to the trauma, and on such factors as inner strengths, imagination, memory, supportive environments and sources of inspiration.

It is not uncommon to find people with various dogmas forming support groups and sympathetic organizations. They become expressions of theater as traumatized people use them to restage their own drama. The trauma can become secondary to the symbolic and metaphoric expressions of their life that are thus being portrayed. Similarly, the doctors, therapists and helpers become part of the theater; indeed they begin to build the theater around themselves for the recurring re-enactment of their self-attributed and acquired roles.

Some argue that the scale of the death makes a difference to the reaction and to the prospects of recovery. There is no doubt that the scale and style of the death do affect us. We express satisfaction that at long last the old man who had experienced months of pain died peacefully in his sleep. On the other hand we are horrified at the brutality of the Holocaust deaths and recognize the distress of those who survived, or had near-miss experiences, or were somehow given an exemption from that ultimate threat that had been placed upon them. We are likely to say that people who went through, or were close to, such terror and horror never get over it. But we then meet some who did! The scale of the death and the nature of the death can deceive us into thinking that death itself is ultimately different, and that somehow we are excused from coping with it and its associated images and memories, and the outrage and disgust that accompany them. While many people may argue that the Holocaust was the worst horror to be visited on a section of humanity and that it was made worse by the inaction and apparent collusion of the onlooker, they overlook the far wider horror of famine in Africa and the indifference of the world to the deaths of so many human beings. Ultimately, is the death of millions of Jews and Gypsies different from the deaths of twenty million Russians in the same war? Is the death of thousands from torture under oppressive regimes different from the deaths of five hundred people in a plane which was blown to fragments by a bomb planted by a terrorist organization? Is the death of millions of Cambodians different from the Jamestown deaths? Ultimately death is death, and the survivors, mourners and onlookers have to cope with the death, recognizing that the scale of the death or the horror by which it is interpreted is secondary to the fact that death is death whatever the circumstances in which it occurs.

We, as a society, tend to bring a trauma consciousness to the events and expectations of life. As the taxi driver was taking me to the airport, his radio was broadcasting low volume the early morning news. When the driver caught one word of the overnight tragedy, he turned the radio to full volume: "A young man shot five of his relatives dead, left two with serious injury, then suicided." Unable to identify with the attacker or the victims, we become horror-struck by the trauma and the way it is repeated from station to nation. A trauma consciousness can so possess us that we perceive that human beings are the inevitable victims of trauma and that their helplessness in the face of such destiny curtails their responsiveness to it. In the context of such thinking a person may deeply and tenaciously feel and function as if they will never recover from their losses. Whether we look at the five hundred killed in a plane disaster, six million in the gas ovens, twenty million in the Russian–German war or sixty million with one nuclear explosion, we are dealing with frightening odds. All the more reason why we should inculcate attitudes of hope, strengthen the human spirit and create environments of beauty, joy and vitality that can change the way of coping with the inner and outer wounds of life.

This book is directed toward such a goal. It is about recovering from loss and grief so that people move back into the full stream of life more quickly than they might have done. We need to find the ways to intercept these post-traumatic stress reactions and disorders and reduce their overt and hidden hazards and heavy costs. I believe it can be done. I have sat with many people who have shown me it can be done. They have also taught me *how* it might be done.

Our task is to make something of our traumas and losses, and our reactions to them. We can drift on in an impaired existence or, like the salmon, we can continue to respond to that which is within us and beyond us, and make the leap, and find it worth the effort as we take our part in the larger scheme of things.

1

Experiences of Grief

> We cannot put off living until we are ready. The most salient characteristic of life is its coerciveness; it is always urgent, "here and now", without any possible postponement. Life is fired at us point blank.
>
> José Ortega y Gasset

Her father had been missing for two days. That in itself was unbelievable. How could her father simply disappear when for all the twenty years she had known him, he had done everything in a predictable, conventional way? In the face of this unbelievable fact, Kate was tangled in the anxiety of an increasingly believable suspicion — that her father had run into some dreadful fate. As she turned her car into the parking lot at the supermarket, a newsflash on the radio reported that a man's body had been found under the Mitchell Bridge. She said she knew at that moment her father had been murdered. The anxiety of not knowing was suddenly converted into a grief that was inconsolable.

Kate had always had a close relationship with her father — at times she thought it was far less demanding than the relationship between her father and her mother. She could not understand why anyone would want to kill him and why they should dump his body under the Mitchell

24

Bridge which was at least fifty-five miles from his normal expected route. She was frustrated that the police could find no evidence to trace the killer or killers and she was constantly on edge with her mother and two brothers as they all went over the event again and again. She longed and fretted to have one glimpse of what happened in the last hours of her father's life. She continuously imagined what happened. She dreamed about it; she cried about it. After two months, her closest friends began to tell her it was time she was getting herself together but this isolated her in her experience all the more. Nothing seemed to help. In fact, Kate did not know where help was needed or what kind of help could bring any change to her experience.

She felt emotionally damaged, out of touch with reality and not wanting to accept the reality that continued to evoke a distressing nausea and a profound helplessness. Her feelings, her thoughts, her mind, her behavior were chaotic and out of control, and she could not envisage living a stable enjoyable life again.

Tom and Mandy were also facing a crisis of a death of a close family member, but the form it took was different from Kate's. I met Tom and Mandy for the first time three days before their six-year-old daughter, Chris, died from a bone cancer. They came to see me because they did not know how to cope with Chris's approaching death. I discovered that Chris's condition had been diagnosed two and a half years earlier, that she had been in the hospital for most of that time and that she had undergone a constant and vigorous treatment program without significant change or any sign of retarding the ongoing destructiveness of the cancer. Chris was Tom and Mandy's eldest child. They had two other children — Robert aged four and Melissa aged two and a half. Tom himself had three married brothers and Mandy a married sister. Both pairs of grandparents were alive and had always actively involved the several families in a positive adhesive network.

As Chris's death drew nearer, no one in the family network emerged as the coping one who would evoke coping in the other family members. In the last week of her life, it was Chris who realized that all her family needed some help. She said to her father, "I'm going to be dying soon. You'd better start telling everybody it's not hurting me anymore." Tom knew that Chris had selected him to help the others cope with her death and with their hurting in their grieving.

Tom and Mandy asked me if I would come with them to see Chris. Her body was almost gone — so it seemed — but her tiny face revealed her awareness of her parents' gentle stroking. She wanted to talk but words had gone; so we talked, as we stood close to her around the hospital bed. Tom and Mandy then told Chris that I would be the person who would stand with them at her grave and that we would be there to wish her a safe journey. For parents who could not cope two days earlier I thought this conversation one of the most important and moving conversations I had ever heard.

Four days later we buried Chris. Mandy took my right arm and I took Tom by his arm, and together we stood over the small grave as I said those words of farewell. Tom and Mandy knew they were not through their experience — not by any means — but they spoke with gratitude for a little life that changed theirs and for a frail and dying girl who taught them what courage could be.

Faced with a traumatic loss, they had made a reorganization in their attitude, their role and their behavior. It was provoked by their dying daughter who had perceived that they had allowed their emotional confusion to conceal the necessary goal of moving from a noncoping attitude to specific coping behavior.

Rex and Joan had three sons — Colin 23, Morris 20 and Alan 18. I met Rex and Joan one month after Alan's death. At midnight on a cold winter's night, he went into the backyard of their home, soaked himself in gasoline and set himself on fire. The explosion of flame shocked Rex and Joan awake. Rushing to their upstairs bedroom window, they looked down at the frantic sight of Alan ablaze. Seized by horror and urgency they ran downstairs to roll him in their blankets. Eventually with the fire out, they realized what had happened. Rex cradled the unrecognizable body of his son in his arms as he groaned and died.

The neighborhood gathered to witness this tragic sight. They all knew that Alan had appeared to be a moody boy but everyone would testify to what a good normal church-going family this was. Rex and Joan had a further concern. They had been to see three doctors and a psychiatrist about Alan. When he turned 15, they noticed a strange change in the boy. He moved in and out of moods that they had never known before. Unlike Colin and Morris, he was very uneven in the way he related to the family, and in the last three years of his life he tended to isolate himself increasingly.

Rex and Joan had enormous difficulty coping with Alan's death and their own grief. Their reaction was complicated by their own involvement — "Surely we must have done something wrong, somewhere" — and by their anger toward those who had not recognized the ultimate destructiveness of the behavior they and Alan had repeatedly described — "Surely they could have seen what this was all about!"

At first they succumbed to a diffuse grief. Relatives, friends and counselors kept suggesting they should "talk about it," presumably assuming that a diffuse grief needed a diffuse ventilation. But the pain and distress were unrelieved. It was necessary to make a distinction between the reality that was now upon them and the suffusion of feelings around so many past events and memories. These did not snap into place, nor did they slowly ease into a better state. They required constant specific attention.

In *Coping* (1985) I have described an acute catastrophic reaction:

Jane, aged twenty-seven, was driving her new Toyota car to work one morning. She was astonished to see a seven-year-old child run across the road, obviously on her way to school. The child had not looked to left or right but had been preoccupied with waving to someone back in the direction from which she had come. In a lightning instant Jane saw the child and the danger in which she had placed herself, and followed her with a glance of dismay. That glance was sufficiently long for the child's four-year-old brother to run across the road in excited pursuit of his sister.

It was only when Jane looked in the rearview mirror to see what she had obviously run over that she saw the four-year-old on the road and his sister running back to him. Jane remembered screaming. In a split second she noted her decision to stop rather than to take flight from the situation. She ran up and down the street in a state of hysteria calling out at the top of her voice.

The adults who reached the scene were totally absorbed in trying to bring the dead child back to life. Three people were having acute catastrophic reactions to what had happened. In addition to Jane there was the mother who had been so involved in helping one of her other children that she had not noticed her infant son escape through the front door. She was shocked, grief-stricken and guilty. Part of her was numb and part was angry at the unknown killer of her child. There was the seven-year-old child who felt that her excitement at waving goodbye to her brother had encouraged him to follow. She experienced shock that she had narrowly missed death herself, unforgettable horror at what she saw on the road, massive guilt and fear over the fact that she knew she had caused it all to happen, and an excessive sympathy for Jane.

In this extraordinary meeting of two people who had never met before and have never met since, the seven-year-old began running up and down the street after Jane. She kept calling to Jane, "Don't worry: it was not your fault." But Jane showed no heed for the child and soon both of them were running up and down the street in a state of hysteria (p. 140).

We need to go on from there to recognize the different types of grieving and coping that we might see in Jane, the seven-year-old, the mother of the dead child, the father and the neighbors.

Those who were most acutely affected may seek some help, and in each case the help will be different. Others, not so much at the center of the tragedy, will probably not seek any help. But some of them might have been deeply distressed by it and may have considerable difficulty integrating the event and its aftermath into their experience and way of being-in-the-world.

I remember my 99-year-old aunt, vigorous, alert and still retaining her well-known sense of humor. She did not hesitate in saying, "It's time for me to die. I've had enough. There's nothing here for me now."

Her family would chide her gently: "We all want you to make a hundred."

But my aunt would laugh and say, "*They* want me to make a hundred, but when you get to my age, it doesn't matter."

When her 60-year-old son suffered a disabling stroke, my aunt said, "The poor poor chap. I just feel so much for him. But he's no good now. It would be better for him to go."

She had seen many deaths. She had developed such an attitude of mind and an orientation to life that death did not intimidate her. For herself it was a delayed but necessary inevitability; for her son she saw it as a desirable relief. Death was not something that stood in stark opposition to life. For her, even its tragedy could be accepted and integrated within her overall philosophy of a providential design.

Juliet in Shakespeare's *Romeo and Juliet* said:

What's in a name? That which we call a rose,
By any other name would smell as sweet.

So death by any name or in any form is death; yet we see how differently it affects us, how differently we perceive it.

Carl and Nora came to Australia from Europe. Their lives had been marked by tragedy and coincidence. As children they had lived as next-door neighbors. They were eight years old when it was clear the Nazi terror would send them all to Auschwitz. Their respective parents hid them under the coal in a huge coal box. When the houses were searched, the neighbor's coal box was emptied out, but the box in which the two children were hidden was not touched. Carl and Nora were terrified as they heard the violent commotion of their parents being taken away. They remained in the box, they thought, for hours without whispering a word. When they emerged, it was dark and everything was silent. They decided to make their way to the home of Carl's aunt across the city. Along the way they ran into another

Gestapo search squad and in the rush to hide they lost each other. They passed through two different German camps and on several occasions came close to losing their lives.

Six years later in the mopping-up of the war, they met again as they waited for hours in line to get aid from a resettlement agency. Carl was told he could migrate to Australia. Nora was to resettle in Holland. They parted and did not keep contact. Conditions in Holland were deteriorating for Nora and she applied for migration. At first, she was offered a possibility in America but this was withdrawn two days before she was to leave. Six months later she was offered a passage to Australia. She took a night cleaning job at a large inner-city school where one evening she ran into Carl who was enrolled for evening classes. A year later they married. They had three children.

I met Nora twenty-six years after she arrived in Australia. Her children were then aged 20, 22 and 25. Carl had become a successful importer. She said he had always been a good husband and a good father. He had developed a terminal cancer in the stomach and would die within six weeks. Nora felt it was impossible to part with him. She was unable to tell him he was dying, for she felt that would betray a relationship that by its history and nature was meant for eternity.

The son and two daughters were in a dilemma. Their father was dying and they felt he ought to know so that he could grieve and take his leave from them all with dignity. Their mother refused to allow them to tell their father he was dying and she rejected all efforts to comfort her or to help her make the preparations for the adjustment that would be necessary. She recalled the tragic circumstances in which she lost her parents, and how

Carl had lost his. From the day in the coal box when they were eight years old, neither of them had heard a single word as to what happened.

"It was as if they were suddenly obliterated from life," she said. "How can I let dear Carl go? He has never had another person to love him, and I am the one who has always loved him." A part of her own world was collapsing and the thought of it overwhelmed her to such an extent that she denied it. But death has little respect for human resistance or denial. Nora tried valiantly to sustain her unrealistic view of life and death, and was unprepared for the ultimate course of events. Her children could see how this affected her judgment, her behavior and her whole way of living.

Lorraine wished her husband were dead. She had married Bruce sixteen years earlier. They had three children aged 8, 10 and 14. It had never been a satisfactory marriage. At first, it appeared that Bruce was carrying his anger and resentment from his previous marriage. Lorraine had married him when he was 41 and she was 31. In retrospect she felt that the age difference may have been a disruptive factor, and perhaps also that she had already established herself in a career and in her ways. She was reluctant to accept that Bruce had a serious psychological problem particularly manifesting itself in the marriage relationship.

They had separated six years before they saw me but this separation lasted only three weeks. Lorraine feared Bruce's homicidal threats and she was worn out by his telephone calls at any hour of the day or night. As soon as the family was reunited, the shouting and the physical pushing and threatening resumed.

Lorraine again left the home, taking the three children. She was determined not to return, even in the face of the threats. Bruce promised to change his ways if only Lorraine would return. When he could see that this had no effect he would burst into violent abuse again. Lorraine and her family have now been separated from Bruce for eighteen months. Sometimes they feel sad for him, but always they are resolved never to return. "If he died, there would be four people who would experience the greatest relief of their lives," Lorraine said.

Lorraine used the death wish as a way of trying to solve a difficult problem. Bruce had so entwined himself into her life by his violent threats, demands and pathetic pleas of dependence and helplessness that Lorraine could not extricate herself — either externally and objectively or internally and subjectively.

Many relationships are not so fraught with overt tyranny but are just as irreconcilable and as irretrievable. The partners within those relationships look to death to bring a solution. They shout at each other: "I wish you would drop dead!" They utter the veiled curse: "One day you'll get your desserts; they'll carry you out feet first and see if I lose any sleep over you!" But there are many others who would recoil from such words, but nevertheless convey the death wish. Sometimes it is recognized, sometimes it is not. Sometimes it is focused outwardly. Sometimes it is subtly manifesting itself in the illnesses and attitudes internally.

The death wish can hinder the resolution of a problem and may confuse and obstruct a person's successful adaptation to a different life-style. This was evident with Beryl.

She knew she was very angry. She felt she had every reason to be. After thirty-three years of marriage Joe had walked out. She said it was outrageous that a woman of her age (she had just turned 60) should be left on her own. All her married life she had worked to look after the children, provide meals and attend to the domestic chores, and just when her husband should be easing back on his commitments and devoting time and attention to her, he packed his things and left.

Did he have another woman to go to? "No," Beryl replied. "In a way that would be easier to accept."

I think she could have meant that then he would be clearly blameworthy, but by leaving her without an obvious external cause he made it look as if she was inadequate or a failure. At times of separation and grief a person's perception of the attitudes of interested audiences can become a major preoccupation. In actuality I have come to realize that interested audiences may have an interest for a very short time, or may not be interested at all. But Beryl could have been attributing to them an interest and views that they did not have.

When Joe came to see me he was adamant that if I had any thought of trying to bring them together for any kind of discussions, I was wasting my time. He said it was true that Beryl had done all the things she said she had done. But he went on.

"She never could appreciate that I always wanted something different in a wife. Her attention to domestic matters did not include tidiness. I lived for thirty years on a junk-heap. I had my job as a professor at the university. That could have been more enjoyable if she had agreed to entertain or join me happily in the entertainment given by other people. But we always — always — had tension in the air about those events.

"From time to time I gave public addresses. It would have been nice if, now and again, Beryl had shown a slight interest in what I was saying. I have written four books and more than forty technical papers and well over a hundred popular articles. I doubt if Beryl has ever picked up one of them in her hands ...

"If she is angry about the way I left, she will just have to be angry. All I can say is it was impossible to have a sensible conversation with her for the last ten years. With all of her buddies, she was charming. She would laugh and giggle on the phone and talk for hours. When I would phone (maybe with the single statement that I would be late home for dinner) as soon as I said 'Hello,' a coldness flowed in my direction. I reached the point that I would not bother to phone her, because I knew what a turn-off it would be. Then she complained that I had not let her know I was going to be late. I reached the point that I preferred no meal at all than to have that kind of tension present each evening."

Beryl had to do the necessary separating from Joe. It involved her anger at his injustice and her denial of his experience. She said, "I wish I could just die. There's nothing to live for, anyway." Her four children — all married — tried to encourage her to get on with her life but she was sullen and resentful and avoided life-affirming activities and acted on the basis of an imagined non-negotiable fusion with Joe who had long since withdrawn from the relationship.

Joe said, "You know, if Beryl died, I would go to her funeral because I recognize her as a person I once contracted into an important relationship. She is also the mother of the same children of whom I am the father. But they are all fully grown mature people. We are not talking about kids. You see, I have lost all interest in Beryl. I have finished that book. There is nothing more coming out of it, and I have nothing more to put into it. Beryl is stuck and will not take the course of being free in herself.

"What I know is this: I can't help her to do what she

herself does not want to do. I can't help her now at all. She alone can decide whether she is going to live the next phase of her life or wither on the vine one way or another."

The death wish can become hidden beneath overt expressions of guilt and shame. It can manifest itself as in King David's statements of "I wish I had died instead" and the many self-punitive broodings of "if only."

John and Susan came to see me because their marriage was breaking down. They felt the major disruptive issue was the death of their 12-year-old son, Andrew, a year earlier.

He had gone on a school camping trip. For three weeks prior to the trip he had tried to persuade his father to let him have an excuse to miss the trip. Andrew's two older sisters chided him and told him it would be great fun. But he insisted he did not want to go. His father was determined he should go — it would "do him good." Andrew went. On the third night of the trip he had an asthmatic seizure, and before anyone realized what was happening, he was dead.

According to John and Susan he had never had any sign of asthma previously, though there was a history of asthma in John's family. His grandfather and his brother had had conditions of an asthmatic nature when they were preadolescent.

John was bereft and guilt-ridden. He argued that he alone was responsible for Andrew's death. He had not listened. He had not leaned toward him. He was only determined on what he thought should happen and, as a result, Andrew had died. If Andrew had stayed at home he would still be alive. Thus he continued to berate himself to anyone who would listen. Susan reassured him that she had been just as involved; that although she had not resolutely said he should go, she had fully accepted John's view and gone along with it without question. No one could have predicted this odd episode that would take his life.

John brooded interminably. He became extremely aggressive and moody until Susan came to the view that it was not only impossible to live with John but that his behavior was destructive and distressing for the two girls and for her. Susan said she knew it sounded selfish, but everyone had to accept the reality that Andrew was dead. There was also the other reality: that she and the girls had a right to go on living. Nothing was gained for Andrew, or anyone, for them to continue their depression and distress.

John said Andrew's death was something he could never forget. He could not forgive himself. He would never get over it. He refused any counseling or therapy. He joined a grief support group which kept him supported in his grief and thus his grief was sustained rather than resolved. When he heard that people he knew were going through a bereavement, he would call them and tell them about his grief. This was still going on seven years after Andrew had died. While John refused to "get over it," he denied the reality that other people were over it. Susan could not forget it but she had remarried. The two daughters were both married with infants of their own. They were building their future in their own context whereas John continued to return to the school camp of so many years earlier.

John remained buried in Andrew's death and entangled in the web of his own death wish. He persisted with his daily self-punishment and his frequent tearful purgings. He was reluctant to acknowledge that his behavior had entrapped him in a life-style that he did not wish to revoke. He could not recognize that the words he was using — "I'll never get over this"; "I can't forgive myself"; "I can't forget that I am responsible" — became the statements of his destiny. When he said, "I'll never get over this," he was not uttering a plea for help; he was making a determinative statement about himself and his future. Some support people agreed with him and endorsed his statement when they said, "You never do get over tragedies like that." No one stopped to examine the meaning of these words. No one realized it was possible to change the words as Susan did and say, "I can't forget it, but I must get over it."

We also need to re-examine what is meant by the words "I can't forget it." These words can gather a power that they need not have. They imply that the memory is a constant burden, always there, always interfering with a person's thinking, functioning and life-style. In actuality, what is meant is that the memory is easily recalled, it is readily accessible, but the person finds that it may be evoked only from time to time. As the memory of the event and the person's involvement in it become more settled within their inner thoughts and attitudes, they begin to use a different way of speaking about it. They may say, "I once thought I would never get over that, but now I'm starting to feel a little bit different about it." The early rigidity has given way to the beginning of some new possibilities. The traumatic loss will always be a significant and remembered event in their life history but it need not dominate their ongoing life story nor preclude them from experiences of happiness and enriched appreciation.

Jacqueline Lowes, aged 21, had been deeply and generously influenced by her stepfather who was a man of significant achievements and warm sensitivity and care.

He died suddenly. In her efforts to express her grief and integrate her loss, Jacqueline wrote this poem that reflects her admiration and appreciation:

Lament

In the darkest hours of mourning night
I weep not for what he could have been,
For his life was divine in its fulfilment.
But the emptiness his departure awakes
is an anguish without relief.
Though, it is said, Time's soft touch may
    someday mellow the panic in my heart,
There can be no more soothing comfort
    than the memory of our beloved,
And the dulcet tones of his modest
    joie de vivre
An overwhelming image of waltzing peace
    and acceptance.

There is so much to be rejoiced in this
    man's proud life,
Where tears seem out of place,
And no attempted description will suffice —
How can one begin to explain such pure
    heart and wise excellence?

"Self reverence, self knowledge and
    self control",
How the words catch in my throat —
No truer ones exist
But even these cannot capture the vitality
    and presence of their master
To whom, through such insight, I owe an
    everlasting debt of nurtured understanding.

When my own selfish pain fades,

And the fear of life without him becomes
    sweet melancholy for the past that
    has passed,
The memory of his presence will be a
    beckoning fire inside me,
In a coveted corner where I will retreat
    whenever life becomes fierce battle
    or insoluble puzzle.
Here there will be no sense of loss or pain; —
Only eternal strength and inspiration,
And clutching gratitude for the
    unconditional gift of his life and love.
What greater joy than sweet tears in
    his name?

(Dedicated to her stepfather, Arthur Gardner)

2

The Language of Grief

If you would indeed behold the spirit of death, open your heart wide unto the body of life. For life and death are one, even as the sea and river are one.

When you are sorrowful, look again in your heart, and you shall see that in truth you are weeping for that which has been your delight.

Kahlil Gibran

Ring out the grief that saps the mind.

Alfred Tennyson

Many of us, as we grieve, commit a gradual suicide. We believe we are rightly grieving for someone who has died, but simultaneously we are not letting ourselves live. We withdraw from life and inhibit its flow. We give up life-affirming activities while we strive to hold onto that false security of an imagined fusion with the person who has left us.

Grieving is only one reaction to separation and loss. As a form of behavior it has gathered around it a variety of accepted modes of conduct and ritualized activity. It is part of most cultures' response to death and dying.

In recent times grieving has been elevated to a skill that everyone should learn, to an approved form of normal behavior. Various studies carried out on how people grieve in various cultures, groups and families have given rise to a number of prescriptions as to how people should grieve. We have been led to believe that grieving is inevitable, universal and patterned to progress from shock to resolution. Grief counselors have sprung into being. Various grief and consolation groups have developed. The funeral industry has spawned intense competition in catharsis and consolation, strongly anchored on the notion that people should grieve, that they should be helped to grieve at a particular time and in particular ways, and that grieving is good. It will prevent health and relationship problems; it will provoke personality growth and promote a deepening spiritual or existential awareness. Many grief and support groups are so strongly supportive that they continue to support the grief rather than the person. As a result, grief is sustained rather than relieved, and the grief encouraged as a way of keeping in some kind of contact with someone from whom contact has been irrevocably lost.

Grief is first and foremost a sign of distress. It indicates that a person is experiencing difficulty adapting to the reality of change and loss. At many points grief seeks to deny the anxiety of the reality of what has occurred and evades dealing with the reorganization that is necessary. It also takes us out of the mainstream of life to become enclosed in preoccupations and regressive activity, in depression and falsification of life's reality. It has become something we owe the dead person, something we owe ourselves, a necessary debt life extracts from us, the survivors.

But there is another side to grieving, especially when we recognize it for what it is: a temporary or permanent form of neurosis from which we must necessarily seek the earliest relief. Grief is not an inevitable reaction to separation and loss. It is but one reaction. It may show itself in the single sigh of a young woman who has just lost her lover to a rival, or it may manifest itself in a diffuse multiphasic, multilateral, multidirectional experience. In some instances of separation and loss, the person experiences great elation, relief and freedom. In other instances the person experiences months of depression and many frustrated and helpless reactions to all encouragement to re-enter life's activities and relationships. We know that some people are relieved when a person dies or leaves; others become deeply traumatized and have no effective way of diminishing their persisting distressing memories.

A great deal seems to depend on the language and metaphor we use when we talk of separation and loss, death and grieving. We hear ourselves say, "He was deeply attached to her." Yet in saying that, we know we are not talking about an attachment in the physical sense as when we take a chain and attach the dog to the fence. We know that when we use the word "deep" we are not talking about a linear dimension, but a depth of feeling, an intensity of dependence or a strength of habitual behavior. We may not have any demonstrable evidence of depth of the attachment. But these words may be chosen by us to describe what we infer from what the survivor has said from time to time. They may have no consensual validity.

We hear ourselves say there was a "strong love between them" as if we could see love, measure its strength and recognize its spatial presence "between" them. Such is the peculiar mystery of human experience that our language is inadequate to describe its subjectivity, its intensity, its tragic disjunction.

"I cannot bear to let him go."

"He's gone, but he'll always be with us."

"Our loved ones, though they are dead, keep us alive."

"I kneel at the graveside, and I can still hear her talking to me."

In grief, our language is about being attached to someone and then the severing of that attachment. It is about
the disruption of an assumed, experienced or imagined
bond. People in their grief talk of losing someone as
if they owned them or possessed them or were so identified with them that they felt part of them. But they are
talking about themselves. They may be talking about
their earliest primal anxiety of being thrust out of the
warmth of the womb into that never-to-be-resolved
existential alienation and loneliness. They are talking of
a trauma they have forgotten or repressed and they are
constantly wanting to deny or defend themselves against
that ultimate anxiety and trauma of their own death.
They are in that realistic flight from the existential life–
death polarity. They want to live yet they are dying. They
reject death but do not know how to secure their living.
They are living but they succumb to death and destructiveness; they are dying but they would fight to stay alive
and maintain productivity. With Dylan Thomas they
might say to the aging father within them:

> Do not go gentle into that good night,
> Old age should burn and rave at close of day;
> Rage, rage against the dying of the light.

Although grief is about distressed feelings and disor-
ganized behavior, ultimately we have to listen to the
language we use to hear how it comes to affect us as it
does. If a father says, "I was very attached to that child,"
we might expect a profoundly distressing grief reaction.
But if he goes on to say, "But I accept what has happened
with the same courage as she showed when she was
dying," we might then expect the grief reaction to be
tempered. If another father shows that his grief is but-
tressed by a persistent anger and self-destructiveness, then

we see that his attachment is not so much to the dead child but to the defenses he adopts to deal with his own imagined omnipotence and ultimate vulnerability.

The language we use reflects how we are grasped by a particular experience and how we would shape it. The language arises from attempts to organize external events and inner experience: the happening and the perception and interpretation of the happening. Thus, although grief is inevitably about the loss of another person (the loss of an object, a part of us or something that had become valued by us) it is primarily and ultimately about inner feelings, inner organization and *our* behavior (not the behavior of the one who has died). Grief, in effect, attempts to hold onto the lost person until the psyche has had time and space to reorganize the grieving person's view of the world, experience and self, with the lost person absent. Some would argue that such reorganization is the grief process. If that is so, then it is important to be more specific about that process.

Freud (1917) said there were three specific phases in the mourning process: the loss of the loved object with the consequent loss of the capacity to invest attachment or energy in the loved person who has gone, the withdrawal of that energy into the self where a reorganization can take place, and a gradual reinvestment of that energy in new objects, people or activities.

We need to examine more carefully what happens in that inner reorganization and how that reinvestment can be accelerated and directed into positive, constructive action. The goal is for rapid relief of grief and the more effective management of persistent traumatic memories. We have been told that grief has a process and that grief has to be worked through. That process has often been left to the grieving person to find, and the working through has been largely a matter of verbal ventilation, recalling memories until they have been drained or desensitized of their traumatic impact, and various purging and cathartic expressions.

I have attempted to map out the grief process in a more productive and effective way to reach the goals of positive change, relief and reorganization. We know that continual rehearsal and review of the loss may be experienced and described by some as helpful, but there may be little healing. We also know that a person can have an exhaustive catharsis and say, "I feel a lot better now," but it may be without a sustained healing. Some people have great difficulty coping with a death experience and grieving because they have never been taught how this difficult life stress can be coped with effectively. After an early spurt of help, we tend to leave these people to cope in the longer term in the best way they can.

People say to me, "Don't you think you are too much concerned with death?" There is a danger that we use such a preoccupation as our way of not affirming life and participating fully in it. But our anxiety about our own death tends to push us away from actually confronting the senselessness of it or the significance of it, the acceptance of it or the utter waste and damage that it sometimes brings.

A friend of mine in his middle eighties sits in his home each day waiting for death. He has inoperable tumors in both lungs, caused in large part from sixty-five years of heavy smoking. In his professional life as an engineer he has had a brilliant career, a distinguished war record and many excellent community achievements and awards. When he retired at 68, there were immediate requests for his services from government and community bodies. For fourteen years after retirement he was fully involved, until his respiratory capacity began to collapse. He says his death is senseless but "I have no alternative but to accept it." He sees it as senseless because over a life-time he has gathered an enormous range of experience and wisdom which at death will be lost. He acknowledges that that was the inevitable life cycle, but on a rational appraisal it seemed senseless. His stoicism reflects his way of living and his way of dying.

Another friend of mine is a 34-year-old woman, divorced and the mother of three children aged five, seven and ten. She has terminal cancer and will die within a year. On the one hand cancer as a disease is kinder than the more sudden traumatic deaths. It gives us time to make preparations for our parting and death. But in cases such as this woman, we can do little more than stand in astonishment at the waste, and the damage it can bring to the young lives of her children. We are not only face to face with the anxiety and tragedy of death in the lives of the family: we are also facing our anxiety over the apparent inconsistent, predatory and fortuitous nature of death and our own powerless and defenseless state. Our perception and our evaluation of the approach-ing death, the words, the language we use, disclose some-thing of our philosophy of life and something of how we will cope with the death.

The sense of powerlessness can become more confused and confounded as separation and death arouse a more primal anxiety. It is extremely difficult to know exactly what occurred between a person and his parents during his infancy years. There is no doubt that many children are left to endure unpredictable or devastating parental separation without interpretation or reassurance. A sense of helplessness and intolerable anxiety force the child to construct a fantasy of omnipotence containing an imagined and permanent bond between the child and the parent. This is an attempt to deal with the vulnerability that the child has confronted within the self.

Psychologists have different ways of describing the various possibilities which may follow. Whether we talk of forming a fantasy bond with the mother, or incorporating the external mother within the self as a safe internal object, we are talking about an internal organization to deal with the child's perception and experience of the external world. We can speculate and sometimes observe that the maneuvers adopted by the child are rarely strong enough to provide that ultimate protection from the wounds of separation and fracturing and fluctuating reality. Robert Firestone (1985) wrote:

> The fantasy bond initially protects the infant against the ravages of its reactions to temporary separations from its mother, separations which it interprets phenomenologically as permanent loss. *Temporary separations from the mother and tentative moves toward autonomy evoke a form of deep anxiety and dread that are the precursors of the unbearable emotional response that is aroused somewhat later by the full awareness of one's death* (p. 243).

Parents frequently underestimate the sensitivity of the child; indeed, their denial of that sensitivity may be related to traumatization during their own childhood. But infants require generous amounts of a lavish and loving presence of parents to help them emerge from their highly protected experience of a very limited world to an acceptance of the peculiar contingencies of the wider world where the comings and goings of parents do not arouse intolerable anxiety and the prospect and occurrence of death do not provoke that state of helplessness and dread.

While this preventive action is emphasized, we nevertheless need to recognize that many adults have such difficulty coping with death and grief because of early disruptive experiences and anxiety during those infant years. Although some might discount the significance of such experiences, clinical work repeatedly attests to it. At times of grief people tend to regress, become helpless, deny reality and deny their own capacity to cope. Grief counselors, clergy, doctors and undertakers may unwittingly collaborate in this regression. Instead of breaking the grief behavior and rumination, there is a strongly held view that grief should take its course, or that it involves a necessary process. There are now documented instances of grief taking its course in such a way that the griever succumbs to illness and may himself die.

Folklore, attitudes and ideas and the many statements about loss and grief need to be placed critically within the context of the necessary goals of recovery and growth, and a commitment to live life as fully functioning, stimulating and healthy human beings.

3

Painful Feelings:
The Goal of Rehabilitation

Only people who are capable of loving strongly can also suffer great sorrow; but this same necessity of loving serves to counteract their grief and heals them ... Grief never kills.

George Vaillant

The death of a loved one is a stark reality that we might like to deny but the external reality is such that part of it, at least, cannot be denied.

A week after the funeral I called on the widow. She said, "Yes, I know we buried John last Tuesday, but he will always be here with me. I just want to leave everything exactly as he left it — that's how he would have liked it."

John's body was cremated. The external observable person was fully and legally removed from the home and from all actual human transactions. But the widow continued to believe he was present, and insisted on preserving the environment that would be conducive to her belief.

Her 40-year-old son faced her with yet another reality. "You cannot continue to live in a large house. Now that Dad has gone, there is no money to keep this house going and you are not able to do all the work it requires." This further encroachment of reality forced her to sell the house and furniture and move into a smaller dwelling within an elderly people's settlement. Gradually she accepted the full reality of her husband's death. Four years later, she remarried. An external reality had been dealt with internally.

This is one of the key issues in the grieving process: That although the grieving person is much preoccupied with the lost object (the person who has died) the real adjustment is not with the external realities and symbols but with the internal organization, which is an activity of the mind.

Feelings of grief can be so distressing and uncomfortable that we do not want to talk about them. We talk about the person who has died, the funeral, the people who made helpful contact — little mention is made of the feelings of grief. We may not be as expressive and demonstrative as the Iraqi family mourning the death of their young children in a bomb raid on their school or as the black South African woman who lost her husband in a confrontation with the police. But although we are not as outwardly demonstrative, we are probably as inwardly affected.

The nature and extent of the emotional reactions depend not only on the culture and the people. They depend on a wide variety of factors such as the relationship existing at the time, the way the death is perceived, the circumstances and the context. Feelings vary from sorrow, sadness and depression, to anger, confusion and emptiness; from guilt for being a survivor to a feeling of fusion with the deceased or with the next of kin.

In its distressing instances death is perceived and experienced as hurtful and damaging. To avoid making a charge on death we skirt the issue.

"Life has dealt me a hard blow."

"It's been a terribly painful time."

"After David went, I was very confused. I could not get going again. It took two years before I began to function."

"Somehow I was aching everywhere inside. I don't know what I would have done without the children. The soreness of it all seemed to be absorbed in my caring for them."

The emotional pain and upheaval affect normal functioning and feelings, relationships and work involvements. The grieving person needs to be rehabilitated emotionally as quickly as possible. This process is inhibited by at least three factors. First, there is a strong desire — a neurotic demand — to remain emotionally damaged. It sustains an illusory contact with the deceased and it becomes a debt we feel we need to pay. Secondly, the grieving person sees that interested audiences almost demand that they behave as if emotionally in pain or injured. Thirdly, the grieving person has never recognized that the goal is emotional rehabilitation. The tendency is to remain virtually trapped in the emotional no-man's-land where security and control are lost.

One man was grieving for his 18-year-old son three years after his death. "Some people say you get over these things with time. I don't know. I think it has become worse as I grow older. I tell myself it would have been different if he had been killed in the war or even on the roads. You can almost understand those sorts of deaths. But there was Craig in his first year of university, a really promising athlete, a good kid who would do a good turn for everyone. Then he gets this terrible melanoma on his shoulder, and he was dead in four months. I tell you I know what David meant when he said of Absalom, 'I wish I could have died instead of you!' I just bleed for that boy, and yet I know it doesn't do one bit of good for me, the wife, the other kids.

"I've become an isolate. I'm in that sort of state that many fellows would take to the bottle. I won't. Thank God I've got a job that I can lose myself in for seven or eight hours every day. The rest of the time I'm a mess. I've even got to the point of being so confused I could be contriving this mess to avoid everybody. But, by God, it is a painful way to do business, I can tell you!"

Emotional rehabilitation is slow — sometimes impossible — if we do not recognize it as the goal that needs to be reached. We can be so entangled with the feelings, the helplessness and the pointlessness of the loss that so much energy is going into the continuous emotional aeration that no plan of action or goals are developed. The task is compounded if the person has an established history of destructive and neurotic behavior. Many people have never been able to identify their feelings and control them satisfactorily. It is common to find deep depressive feelings confused with anger; a strong conscience to be caring, in conflict with self-immolation. Thus a person may cry ostensibly because he is hurt and feels vulnerable and sad, but the same crying may be an expression of rage turned back on the self. Instead of hurting or destroying the hated object, the person shows he is deeply hurt and wounded so that the hated object will then feel obliged to revoke their stand and become sympathetic and helpful.

A man in his middle years was demonstrative and caring toward his wife and four daughters. They perceived that he was financially successful and able to be caring in more ways than one. The man himself was driven by a strong internal conscience to do all he could for his wife, who was like a mother, and his daughters, who had become more like siblings to him. When he amply cared for them and they were responsive, he felt good, but there was no end to it. He did not recognize that all his caring was in fact a way of dying. He was sacrificing his own life, enjoyment and full actualization by his chronic need to please his wife and daughters.

Walter Kaufmann (1973) wrote:

What makes people inauthentic (and what makes their talk of food and clothes and petty failures and successes so utterly pathetic) is not that they have forgotten they must die before long. It is that they have forgotten that they are survivors (p. 231).

How will emotional rehabilitation be achieved? The task is complicated. We cannot see our feelings or the damage done to them as we can see a damaged limb and the damage done to it. We can more confidently say of a person who has suffered a physical injury: "This person will need to go through a rehabilitation program to get the limb functioning again, so that he can return to an effective role in society."

When a person goes to jail or war, we again use the word "rehabilitation" in the sense of devising programs which will facilitate that person's reinstatement in society and their successful role and position within it. But whereas the rehabilitation programs following World War II were designated successful, programs following the Vietnam War were more commonly designated as failures. Questions have been asked as to whether such programs could be successful in the present climate of knowledge and experience without taking careful cognizance of these people's feelings and how they might be emotionally rehabilitated.

More attention — at least in word — is being given to

emotional ventilation and emotional recovery following traumatic experiences of horror, loss and dislocation caused by bushfires, hijackings and cyclones. But actual programs of emotional rehabilitation have remained elusive or have been dispatched to the too-difficult basket.

The basic emotion is anxiety. That anxiety, when out of control, destroys the inner sense of security, satisfaction and pleasure. It brings disorganization, deprivation and pain. In concentrating on the deceased or the funeral or the loss of the object, we fail to address this anxiety. It disrupts the coherent sense of self, sabotages self-esteem and self-efficacy. Although the actual loss of a significant person often has the consequence of changing one's view of self, of life and of the world, this anxiety places that consequence even further out of control. It disrupts a person's way of functioning, impairs the resistance resources and scrambles those accumulated — albeit uncoordinated — assets for positive living.

A 48-year-old mother from an obscure country town phoned to ask if I would see her and her husband. I had not met her before but the matter was extremely urgent. I arranged to see them on the next day. It was obvious from their faces that they were greatly distressed. As soon as they sat down in my office they both began to cry. Their eldest child, a 19-year-old daughter, had left home to go to a large city university. She was the pride of the extended family as they all anticipated she would be their first member to graduate from a university. She had over-dosed on heroin and had died suddenly. The parents' anxiety was mixed with incomprehension, shame, helplessness and despair. Everything for them had collapsed and they themselves had collapsed and were unable to organize their thoughts, their relationships or their functioning. They felt that although they had coped with many serious difficulties and setbacks in their life, this was beyond them. They had no resistance to deal with such a devastating blow and life was no longer worth living. "I feel like taking the gun and shooting the whole lot of us," the father said.

Emotional rehabilitation was vital to return this couple to an effective level of coping. It would be easy to speculate that they would not ever get over this tragedy, that they would harbor immense anger for their daughter and murderous rage for the person who supplied the drug, and for every drug pusher.

I have seen several parents who have attempted to deal with their anger by becoming identified with helping agencies. While this may be valuable humanitarian work it does not, in itself, do the work of emotional rehabilitation. The anxiety may not have been brought under control.

Emotional rehabilitation involves a distillation process as we identify and trace the disruptive action of the basic anxiety, separated from the secondary emotions of anger, guilt, shame, depression and internal frustration. First, we are confronted with the anxiety of fate and death, of our brevity and mortality, of endings — slow and sudden. Secondly, it is an anxiety reminiscent of earlier losses, sometimes repressed, sometimes regressive, but it is responsive to current traumas and may be an active ingredient in them. Thirdly, the anxiety is the anxiety of meaninglessness and emptiness, of helplessness and futility, of vulnerability, dread and despair. These three streams of anxiety pour their distressing flood into the self — the existential anxiety, the anxiety of early separations and the anxiety of the actual death event — and in the center is the self, struggling desperately to find some acceptable, effective way to cope when, in many instances, nothing seems acceptable or effective.

I set out for grieving people what is required for their emotional rehabilitation. When it is expressed sensitively and empathically they quickly see it as the necessary and urgent course of action. I use various images to help them recognize what is happening, though I point out that no image or analogy can adequately express what is happening. It is like a limb being severed — the blood gushes forth. Unless it is halted, the person rapidly bleeds to death. It is like a river rushing across the plains in full flood. Unless preventive action is taken, it washes everything and everyone along with it. It is like a stampede of people — it can be extremely destructive, leaving casualties and devastation behind it. The basic anxiety is so difficult to cope with because it threatens our established sense of control, it threatens our accepted view and meaning of things and it threatens to be so diffuse that it eludes attempts to convert it into manageable problems and challenges.

I set about to help the grieving people separate the basic anxiety from the secondary emotions that have become entangled with it. Together we decide which we will deal with first: the basic anxiety or the secondary emotions which are specifically designated.

In the family where the 17-year-old boy had committed suicide the week before his final school examinations, we decided it was necessary to deal first with the secondary emotions of the anger the mother had toward the father, and the murderous rage the father had toward the dead boy. They could not face the basic anxiety of the meaninglessness and futility of the death until they had acknowledged they were still powerfully waging a war that they could not see had been devastatingly lost. Their interpersonal conflict seemed to give them a way of avoiding the reality of the boy's death and its significance for the whole family.

Rehabilitation involves identifying the emotion and the extent of its potential and actual damage. The question then is whether we let that emotion be expressed or whether we work to control it, or both. Do we let the patient bleed or do we get the patient bandaged as quickly as possible? Do we let the patient repair to his bed or do we get him back on his feet? There is a well-established view that the grieving person should let it "hang out"; that he should be permitted to talk it through and cry it through — ad nauseam, if that seems to promise relief. I do not adhere to this view. Successful rehabilitation does not depend on emotional ventilation and exhaustion. Ventilation and exhaustion frequently inhibit the rehabilitation.

I am not advocating a suppression and stifling of all feeling. I advocate identification of the feeling and its constructive management and rehabilitation, lest the person is left unnecessarily damaged and rendered ineffective as far as the functional affirming, celebrating aspects of living are concerned.

Resistance Resources

Rehabilitation requires building up resistance resources, and the practiced rehearsal to become emotionally responsive again. Many people become so traumatized by death and grief that they continue to fear their vulnerability. They have few identifiable resistance resources to deal with their basic anxiety. They may withdraw their participation, become frozen in their feelings and expressionless in their way of being in the world. Alternatively they may frequently revert to their grief; only a mention of the dead person, a photograph or some apparently insignificant action may precipitate a collapse of normal functioning. Some people strive to be like Martha in a play by Camus, *Cross Purpose*. After she had killed her own brother she said to her brother's wife:

And now — before I go, let me give a word of advice; I owe it to you, since I killed your husband. Pray God to harden you to stone. It's the happiness He has assigned Himself, and the one true happiness. Do as He does, be deaf to all appeals, and turn your heart to stone while there still is time.

Resistance resources help the person cope with the anxiety of grieving and provide an increasing level of immunity to the potentially devastating and recurring invasion of that anxiety. People caught in grief readily believe they have lost all resistance. They have become victims and the grief is their load to carry. I encourage grieving people to focus on specific resistance resources:

1 Rebuild the sense of self, the sense of who you are, your self-confidence. After the first impact of grief, this objective seems impossible. But beginning from even minimal foundations, we begin to rebuild this vital resource:

"I am Peter's mother … I am Joanne's mother."

"My friend Alice called me today. My friend. Alice treats me as her friend. I have Alice as a friend."

"I live in Bayswater Road. The dog and the cat always know me. They know who I am. I know who I am. The grief makes me feel dreadful, but I still know who I am. Every day I practice rebuilding the full sense of who I am and who I'll be. I get stronger every day ... I gather strength as I go ..."

2 Give yourself time and permission to grieve. You do not evade the expression of your grief. Purposely plan fifteen minutes each day, to sit in quiet meditation and think on the one who has died. If you feel sad at the loss and the pain, allow yourself to feel the sadness and the pain. If you want to express your gratitude and love, do that. If you feel cheated and angry, acknowledge that. When the time has expired, stand up, breathe in a readiness for the next task and proceed. This time of planned and scheduled grieving also contributes to your growing sense of regathered self and a recovery of security and control.

3 Acknowledge the basic anxiety. Acknowledge the specific secondary emotions. Practice converting at least some aspects of the basic anxiety or the secondary emotions into manageable problems with specific goals. Flooded by helplessness, you can select one area where you need not be helpless. You designate tasks and goals. You work toward these, taking care to evaluate what progress you make.

4 Designate those areas of life where a coherent view is possible. The death or loss provokes a diffuse anxiety where meaning and worthwhileness seem to vanish totally. Practice selecting areas of your life (for example, your work, a special relationship, your friendships in an organization) where you can say, "That makes sense. That is worthwhile. It may not help my sense of loss, but in itself, it is an experience I value."

5 Develop your capacity to recognize that the anxiety associated with death and grief can spread diffusely

into all areas of life. Practice intercepting the spread.

6 Recognize that the basic anxiety can convert into several secondary emotions, and that these secondary emotions can hide the basic anxiety and confuse the management of it. Practice your capacity to separate the basic anxiety from the secondary emotions, and develop the capacity to prevent one converting into the other or one confusing the other.

7 Recognize that the anxiety and the secondary emotions are likely to recur. Practice identifying situations and stimuli that provoke their recurrence. Instead of accepting this as an inevitability, practice early intervention.

8 Focus on symbols that remind you of the processes of rebirth, renewal and restoration. These symbols may be the flowering of springtime, the sunrise, the incoming tide. They may be the symbols of religion and church, of order out of chaos, resurrection after a crucifixion.

9 Cultivate positive restorative images with your experience of music and literature. Practice meditation where life-affirming images are used.

10 Nurture at least one significant supportive relationship. Many feel that this kind of support should be found in the marriage or family relationship. This may not always be appropriate. It is important to recognize that spouses and family members may be responding to the same event in different ways. There may also be some unrecognized feelings between the family members. For such reasons, you might consider carefully which relationship would be most supportive.

11 A person's resistance resources are enhanced as he

develops a commitment to get through the grieving, a commitment to a positive outcome and a commitment to an image of himself as a coping, constructive person. This commitment may be fairly feeble at first but even the smallest indications of it should be identified and confirmed.

12 Practice putting yourself in situations where you can feel alive and spontaneous once again. Play music, encourage yourself to dance, walk in the park, take a holiday. Practice accessing your feelings — the positive, creative, flowing feelings of life. Move more and more into life-affirming pursuits and practice feelings that are appropriately congruent with those pursuits.

4

The New Reality

To live is to suffer, to survive is to find meaning in the suffering.

Gordon Allport

Grief can be so pervasive and overwhelming that it can be with us every day like a chronic illness. The one thing that would relieve it would be to cancel out the loss or the death that has occurred. If only all that had not happened! Unfortunately, that is magical thinking. If someone has left or died, that is the reality. We would like to deny that reality and avoid its many consequences.

It seems that the dead person is keeping us in our grieving and inhibiting any movement toward getting on with life. The attachment or bond we feel with the dead person and our reluctance to relinquish that attachment or bond can also keep us in our grieving. In effect our grieving is our lingering way of keeping the bond alive, though at the same time, our grieving is meant to be a way of severing the bond.

In many experiences of grieving the person is unconsciously dying to be with the dead person and yet they cannot die. They do not want to get on with living, for

63

that not only means leaving the dead person behind, it means actively separating from them. It seems like an act of disloyalty, carrying with it a great deal of apprehension that the dead person is watching them and witnessing their perfidy and the capriciousness of their commitment and affection.

A mother driving her three daughters home from a school sporting event one Saturday afternoon collided with another car and two of her daughters, riding in the backseat of the car, were killed. The mother told me everything was right — the children had won their team event, they were happily planning what they would do that evening. She had right of way through the intersection. In a split second before the impact, she saw the red car. She believed she heard Jenny call out just before they were hit. The red car, traveling at high speed, sliced their car in two. The two girls in the backseat were crushed and killed, while the mother and the other daughter in the front careered out of control and came to a stop a hundred yards along the footpath. Neither of them suffered a scratch.

For months the mother grieved. She would not let her two daughters go. She felt that at their young ages of 15 and 16, she had deprived them of life, marriage, motherhood and maturity. Everything she did was an act of further betrayal. How could she ever enjoy life again when she had deprived them of everything? Nothing could persuade her that she should stop punishing herself. She rehearsed the collision and ruminated on it several times daily. If only there had been a fraction of a second difference in the timing of her entry into that intersection. If only she had quickly swung the car, or maybe accelerated. If only!

Her surviving daughter, aged 13, was shocked and

dazed by the whole event. At first she said it was one terrible nightmare, but after the funeral it suddenly struck her that she and her mother had been involved in a dreadful catastrophe. Given the fact that they were there at that moment, nothing could have been done to avoid it. She and her mother had been the lucky ones to survive as they did.

She told me: "There's no point in me walking around like Mother does, as if I'm also dead. No, I want to live life more now than ever before, because I almost lost it. It sounds selfish, but it isn't really. I think it is admitting what has happened and somehow being grateful that I'm alive."

I was astonished at such words from a 13-year-old, but I have seen several such instances where a catastrophe touches an extraordinary wisdom in young people.

Somehow this 13-year-old was able to find her way to taking the catastrophe realistically into her experience. She was able to decide to be a fully functioning person. But the mother became trapped with the images of her two dead daughters and could not integrate the event into her experience. She showed strong resistance to life and the people wishing to affirm her life.

In another family, the fourth child died at the age of three years. There were three older children, aged five, seven and ten years. I did not meet any of the family until three years after the death, when the parents brought the middle child, then aged ten, for assessment. He was a sullen, undersized young fellow. He had been very destructive at home and had been stealing small items at school. He was a social isolate both at home and at school. During the first meeting with the parents, I learned also of the death three years earlier of their other child. It was evident from our discussion that both parents were still angry and blaming each other for various aspects of that child's death, that their own relationship was fragile and that there were high levels of impatience and fear regarding their other three children, particularly David, the ten-year-old. I asked to see the whole family together rather than David on his own.

During the second session the eldest boy, Tony, aged 13, spontaneously declared that all the trouble dated back three years to the death of Jonathan. He said, "We (meaning his brother and sister) saw Jonathan before he died and we saw him after he died. But that was ages ago. Mother and Dad keep mentioning his name. We can't even remember what he looked like. In fact Jonathan is just a word to us — I think we even hate the word."

At that, his mother began to cry and the father castigated Tony for speaking so coarsely. David was smiling. In this family the children were wanting to leave the dead boy behind and get on with their living, but the parents were continuing to use the name of the dead boy as a current reality in family interaction and manipulation. It was difficult to know what reality each of them was perceiving as important, until David's behavior became so unmanageable that he became the target person for correction. In fact the whole family was entangled in realities that no one could adequately define or discuss.

At times the realities are not only confused but they become part of a public and private deception. Bill and Madge had been married for twenty-two years. They had two children, aged 17 and 19. For twelve of their married years Madge had sustained a private relationship with Maurice, who was also married with two children. They had decided not to break their marriages, ostensibly because of Bill's job and their responsibility to the children. Neither Bill nor Maurice's wife knew anything of the relationship between Madge and Maurice.

At the age of 46 Bill had a massive coronary and died. Madge was at first shocked then privately relieved. She went through the public mourning at the funeral, but she was pleased that at long last her sexual deception was over and that she was now free to pursue her relationship with Maurice on different terms. It then struck her that now Bill was dead, he may have acquired a new capacity to see what she had been doing all of these years. At first this provoked a great deal of guilt but then she laughed and said, "Why should I bother about Bill? He was never anything more than a pathetic observer. I'm going to get on with it, and dump all that spiritualist trash that some people swallow!"

Maurice had another view. His public attitude was sympathetic and supportive. Privately, he was angry that Bill had died, and very frightened of Madge now that she was so aggressively free. He wondered how he would feel if his wife died. Then recognizing that he was the same age as Bill, he floundered a little and wanted to get back to work.

But we ought not to forget Madge's two daughters. Although Madge was relieved and pleased that Bill had died, the two daughters were deeply grieving for a father who had been such a close and significant person for them. Madge had not expected their tenacious distress and it became a further complication in her relationship with Maurice.

Sooner or later most people come to cope with the death and loss of significant people. Sometimes that coping is confused and clumsy; at other times it is courageous and deliberately constructive. Often people do not pause to make any choice: they cope or they make hard work of their coping. In some instances of catastrophe and tragedy the family may find valuable public coping through the medium of their religious commitment or the courageous or distinguished service of the one who died. Privately, the reality is more complex and more difficult to manage.

Constructive coping involves staying in tune with reality. But the reality is often confusing and elusive. It can be a simple acknowledgment that one chapter of life is closed forever, or it can be as complex as being thrown into the captain's seat of a jet aircraft just after takeoff and being told to fly it.

Constructive coping with reality requires a capacity to recognize the reality of the loss, the reality of one's immediate reaction, the reality of the delayed stress reaction, the reality of a recurring stress reaction. It also involves an appraisal of one's resources at the time of the loss and the changing character of one's resources at different times. Reality must also take account of earlier coping experiences, the nature of the environment and the kinds of resources that are available in that environment and how they are perceived to be relevant.

No person is alone in coping with loss and death. We are always part of an environment, always connected with resources. Resources may be available and accessible. The environment may be friendly and supportive. But if the grieving person does not recognize them as such, or is closed off to them, then their value is, to a large extent, lost. High levels of emotional arousal may disrupt and confuse the grieving person's perception of the stress, themselves, their resources and their environment, and also inhibit constructive coping with the stressful situation.

The "new reality" involves a committed and candid attempt to look at what has happened and what is now likely to happen. Many veer away from this task because of its implications of ultimately accepting life without the person who was previously present. At the outset the grieving person has to confront the issue fairly bluntly: do you want to get over your pain, your pining, your distress, your grief? On the one hand they say categorically that they do; on the other hand they conceal their unspoken demand that they would like to get over it but without losing the person they would prefer to keep.

Loss and death change everything. Many people tell me death is easier to cope with than separation and divorce. Death, they acknowledge, is final and ultimate; divorce and separation sustain the awareness that the lost person is still around, that some relationship may be possible and that feelings (both positive and negative) are still active.

With loss and death a change has occurred both in the external environment and the inner experience. A reappraisal is required to take full cognizance of these changes, but the reappraisal is also of one's self, the feelings, the resources, the direction, the reorganization and the new way of being who and how they will be in the next phase of their life. Many widows suddenly realize they have no knowledge of financial management, yet they are left to make decisions on property and investments. At first they might feel inadequate and overwhelmed. With a rational reappraisal they quickly recognize that they can seek advice, that they too can develop skills appropriate to this situation.

One widow I know was left in her husband's will the family home and $20,000. There were also some retirement and death insurances that amounted to $150,000. She was 63 years of age and for the whole of the marriage had been fully dependent on her husband for all financial management. She had no bank account of her own and had never made any bank transactions. She told me she was determined not to fall into "a helpless heap as many women do," so she sought advice from several quarters. She laughed and said, "I've become quite good at playing the stock market. Now at 73, I am worth over a million and half dollars — I've done far better with that money than my husband ever did with any of his money. Yet he always thought I was a bit stupid when it came to money. So I was. I had never learned. But that didn't mean I had no capacity to learn!"

Her "new reality" took her much further. She said, "I now see that life as it was lived with Bob was very limited. He was always saying there was never enough money for this or that, and I never questioned it. Life now is so different. I feel in far better health. I feel so confident. And there are very few limits. That's all because I took sharp stock of myself and I said, 'Now I can't just sit here. If I can do it — with really no education — then I'm sure anyone can do it!'"

The "new reality" means an active perception of the situation and an equally active evaluation and interpretation of it. It is not a passive process. Many people can do it subliminally or intuitively, but constructive coping calls for conscious activity. When John says, "I feel terrible now that Betty has died," he is describing the feeling he has. He has made an appraisal of the inner sensation and experience and he has labeled it "terrible." A reappraisal may reveal that the "terrible" label relates to his loneliness and helplessness, rather than to the blow in the stomach another person may be describing. John's feeling may arise from his apprehension that he does not know what to do with himself, what to do about the children, nor what to do about Betty's aged and ailing mother who has been living with them for the last four years.

It is not the loss that makes John feel terrible. It is his perception and appraisal of the loss that provoke him to label his feeling "terrible." A reappraisal of his realities changed his label. He said, "I see now that when I said I was feeling terrible, I was really confused, angry and even desperate. And of course there was part of me that was so utterly shocked that Betty should die before her mother. We'd always talked about 'when Ma goes,' but suddenly I found that Betty had gone and Ma — who, by the way, is a terrible burden and a terrible nuisance — is still here! As soon as you laid it all out in front of me I began to take a fresh look at everything."

I was interested to note my own reactions at the time of my father's death. He had lived a full, strong and healthy life all his days. He had put his unique mark on life and on those who were closest to him. He died in his mid-eighties, suddenly and unexpectedly. He had been a very significant person in a positive way to us. His death was accepted and integrated into our experience in a short time, with adequate recognition of the kind of person he had been and of the frustration and appreciation to which he had so liberally contributed.

When my bulldog, Dugald, died at the age of 12, we recognized his death as appropriate, expected and a relief from the distress he had suffered. Yet my reaction was far more marked and took longer to integrate into ongoing experience. In both cases, we were dealing with death and loss. In one instance we had the death of a father; in the other, the death of a dog. My appraisal of the events was different and my reaction was different. And my reappraisal was also different. My father had not lived in my close proximity for several decades. The dog had been part of my daily environment for twelve years.

In our management of loss and death and their delayed and recurring stresses, we are likely to label the experience in a certain way as a result of an intuitive or considered appraisal. One father, lamenting his infant son's death twelve years earlier, said, "I owe it to that child. He was my son. He'll always be my son. You just can't walk away from that."

A widow of eight years visits the grave of her husband and places flowers on it. I know that their marriage had been unsatisfactory for several years, but she said, "It's the least I can do for him now." During their marriage she had not bought him a single flower, nor had she picked one from her garden to give him, but each Sunday after his death she has spent money she could ill afford on flowers that would wither in a day on his grave. A reappraisal of her realities is called for: her husand can no longer express any gratitude for the flowers; she provides the flowers to appease her own inner distress; she cannot afford to spend the money on flowers; her new phase of life cannot be lived in the cemetery around her husband's grave; it is eight years since he died; she is now 69 years old; she could have ten more years to enjoy life and affirm its new purpose for her. As she makes this reappraisal, her inner experience will change and her reaction and behavior will change.

She, and the father of the son who died in infancy, had believed they were necessarily reacting to a catastrophe that fate had visited on them. In reality their reaction was contingent upon their appraisal of the event of the death in each case, just as my reactions to my father's death and my dog's death were contingent upon my appraisal of the death in each case. A reappraisal involves a fresh evaluation of the event, the resources available and the meaning the future can have now that the loved object is no longer living or present. The reappraisal asks: "How will I live fully now that that loved object has gone and my life and circumstances, present and future, are inevitably changed?"

In some instances the loss of the loved person means loss of safety and security, belonging and love, and the support, or the illusion of support, that person provided. In the "new reality" the person may need to evaluate if, and how, those needs will be nurtured now that the person has gone and how their higher needs of self-esteem and self-actualization will be meaningfully articulated and actively confirmed and satisfied.

The "new reality" carries the goal of moving from being a temporarily disabled or nonfunctioning person to being a fully functioning person, strengthened and broadened by their appraisal of the life and death of the person who has gone. The fully functioning person emerging from grief might reflect these characteristics:

1 They have developed a flexible capacity to accommodate and integrate antagonistic tendencies into their experience without becoming anxious or alarmed. They can recognize their strengths as well as their vulnerabilities, their search for dependence and their enjoyment of their autonomy, their quiescent reflective moods and their surging demanding passions. They are selfish and unselfish, hardworking and playful, conventional and unconventional, humorous and serious, highly reliable and sometimes unrealistic and unpredictable.

2 They are able to convert their mood states into specific problems that can be solved. When they are depressed, they can evaluate the reasons and circumstances of that depression and recognize that

they can withdraw from the situation, confront some aspects of it or involve themselves in specific activities which may run in parallel to the depression or be a distraction from it.

3   They devise ways to nurture their own self-esteem and self-actualization. They can enjoy their own solitude. They foster their own self-determination as well as their sense of control over the events of their lives, and more especially the appraisal of the events and appraisal of their resources.

4   They develop a strong social interest and participate in social relationships exercising a responsibility in shaping events and attitudes that affect them and their social and family network.

5   They have a warmth and spontaneity about social and creative situations. They might respond joyously to a sunrise or a sunset, but at the same time they have a changing and deepening sense of what they can expect from life and what they will give to it.

5

Ways of Thinking

> We cannot force ourselves to accept ourselves. We cannot compel anyone to accept himself. But sometimes it happens that we receive the power to say "yes" to ourselves, that peace enters into us and makes us whole, that self-hate and self-contempt disappear, and that our self is reunited with itself. Then we say that grace has come upon us.
>
> Paul Tillich

At times of loss and grief our ways of thinking can be disrupted and distorted so that coping is greatly impeded, our capacity to grasp the new reality is affected and our sense of vulnerability is magnified. Often enormous energy is expended on negative self-evaluation, and self-punishment, or on negative ruminations over the past and negative apprehensions and images of the future. These ways of thinking affect how we feel and how we function; they affect our way of being, our life-style and our health. An early goal is to recognize how our ways of thinking about our loss and grief can be an *additional* problem. Our ways of thinking can compound the original problem, exaggerate and expand its significance and delay its effective management. Everyone can develop an awareness of what they are doing in their thinking and they can begin to put into operation some new ways of thinking. Well-traversed, well-learned, habitual ways of thinking are often difficult to change, and the pain and preoccupation of the loss strive to take precedence over the goal of regaining control and finding an appropriate form of coping.

In our ways of thinking we make the important distinction between the identifiable stressor and the way we perceive it — what we think about it, how we appraise it, interpret it and give it meaning, and what we tell ourselves about it. A terrible event for me may be seen by you as common, manageable and nothing to be alarmed about. When I look more carefully at the event, I might see there is nothing I can do to change the situation but my imagination and memory, my apprehensions and predictions of dread, keep gathering strength. I find I have a capacity to draw others into my ways of thinking, and before long, a group of people by their sympathy or agreement give validity and confirmation to my fears.

Our ways of thinking are affected by our memories and images, the stories that are told, the fantasies and the speculations.

"If only your father had not done that ..."

"He'll never get over it ..."

Our ways of thinking can also come to determine how we manage ourselves and the ongoing events of life.

"Ever since that happened, I can't do anything about my feelings. They flood everywhere. There's not a thing I can do about it."

"I can't get over the fact that I could have done something, and I didn't do it. Nothing can change that. I'm stuck with it."

Honoré de Balzac once wrote, "There are no little events with the heart. It magnifies everything ..." Part of a new way of thinking is to recognize how such magnification takes place and how it can be rationally and emotionally intercepted. One event can become an implacable catastrophe, or we continue to give it catastrophic dimensions by saying, "It's the worst thing that could have happened" or "It's the end of everything" or "Nothing can help me now." Along with that we are likely to minimize our own strengths, the good experiences, the positive aspects of the situation. We make overgeneralizations about our ability, performance or worth, on the basis of single incidents. An event is seen as all-or-nothing; it is totally good or totally bad — usually the latter. And we have a readiness to make the matter specific and personal: "Why have I been singled out? Have I not suffered enough already? What have I done to deserve this?"

A new way of thinking identifies these distortions and specifically helps at each point, so that the person gathers more accurate information and perspective, is able to correct faulty beliefs and attitudes, and develops more constructive ways of responding to the distressing events.

Memory can be loaded with sentiment and emotion, with gathered entangled beliefs, and connections with other events which may be part of a larger distortion. Memories, thinking and emotions can become part of a socio-physiological-somatic reaction.

Every time Norma remembers Bert, she becomes miserable and frightened: miserable that Bert has now been dead for five years and she has no one to live with and no one to talk to; and frightened of the future, the dark and herself. She spends a great deal of time cooking and eating. She is apathetic and grossly overweight; she never exercises. She smokes forty cigarettes a day and her blood pressure is constantly well above a level that could be safely regarded as normal.

When challenged about her repetitive compulsive destructiveness, she denied it. She said, "I've always loved cooking. I don't have anyone to cook for now. I remember what Bert used to like so I cook him his cakes. Then of course someone has to eat them; you can't waste them. So I eat them, then I feel dreadful; but soon it starts all over again. It's my way of keeping his memory alive."

She saw her heavy apathy and high blood pressure as the normal conditions and problems of a middle-aged woman. Enabling her to adopt a new way of thinking involved supplying accurate information and helping her evaluate and interpret that information. She had to recognize that she had a problem in letting Bert go. To that she had added her physiological-somatic behavior and condition. The two had become entangled, but had to be drawn apart.

I often tell people that the problem and its emotional loading are like a beetle and its carapace. If the image is not too unpleasant to conceive, we can visualize separating the beetle from its carapace. Imagine the beetle as the problem to be solved; the carapace is the emotional loading we lay upon it. That loading can be so heavy that we cannot deal with the problem or the emotions. We make a separation, so that we deal first with one then the other.

In grieving there are several basic problems and tasks to manage (funeral, family arrangements, finances) but these can become too difficult if we are overwhelmed by distress, anger or guilt. With each situation we decide which we can deal with effectively — the problems and tasks, or the emotions. We might decide to defer dealing with the emotions: in image and word, we place them to one side (not swept under the carpet or bottled up) while we attend to the problems and tasks (or vice versa). When the problems have been attended to, we then focus on the emotions. Sometimes we find they have dissipated in the process of controlling and dealing with the tasks.

In a similar way, we turn attention to the physiological-somatic issues. There is always a close interaction and reciprocity between mind and body in confronting severe stress. Our way of thinking involves developing an awareness of our body image, how it is and how we would like it to be; and what we are trying to communicate to ourselves and others in body image and body states.

In problem-focused coping we designate the problem; we generate possible courses of action; we decide what course of action might be followed, together with the actual action; we might rehearse the action in trial runs; we then take the action into the real situation.

With emotion-focused coping we must again determine what emotions are present in their manifest and concealed or latent forms. We then decide whether the emotion should be verbalized and its expression facilitated, or whether it should be inhibited and controlled. We can devise strategies that block the emotion and the intruding ideas that precede it or that are associated with it, or we can choose strategies that distract us from arousal, impact and expression of our emotions.

In both problem-focused coping and emotion-focused coping we are able to withdraw to give us time to adapt. We are able to see that a diffuse problem or emotion can be reduced or broken into manageable parts. We can recognize that we do not stand or endure on our own, and that the impact and management of the stress are changed as the person uses their belonging to a particular group. But if they feel isolated, misunderstood and without any system of support, their reactions can be much more pronounced. A great deal depends on the self-image that is identified and selected. If grieving people see themselves as self-contained and self-sufficient, their reactions will be different from those who see themselves as deeply dependent or rationally interdependent.

Time-perspective plays an important part in our ways of thinking. People who take the short-term view may see the loss as totally and absolutely devastating. Those who can take the long-term view begin to recognize that death and loss can be integrated into experience and can contribute to adaptive changes in their self-image. Their view is of life and the world, and their capacity to adopt altered states of consciousness and control.

When people receive distressing news of a sudden loss of a job or a death of a loved person, they generally indicate how much the news knocked them off balance.

"I was completely bowled over."

"You could have knocked me down with a straw."

"I was rocked to the foundations."

"Everything was going along so smoothly, then this news came."

"I was shattered."

"I didn't know which way to turn."

"I was completely beside myself."

All of these expressions convey that the once stable state has been disturbed, that the equilibrium in the self and between the self and the world has been upset, at least temporarily. This calls for an inner reorganization to cope with the news and some form of active repair or reconstruction to restore the sense of equilibrium.

As the news of a death is received, several shifts are likely to take place in the person's inner experience. There is the shift from the image of peace and harmony existing between the self and the world, to an awareness that that harmony has been disrupted and the self-image changed. The previously held self-image of belonging and being loved shifts to being bereft and abandoned. There is a shift from feeling in touch with and in possession of a competent comfortable self-image to a self-image that is experienced as decimated, incompetent and defective. I have seen numerous people who have given every appearance of having a strong and competent self-image while the relationship with their spouse was positive, but when that relationship was disrupted it appeared that a dormant negative, worthless self-image suddenly emerged. This shift has far-reaching effects on the person's capacity to cope.

We should not be surprised to find that we all can have this shift from a strong coping self-image to a troubled noncoping self-image. For a time this incompetent and helpless image may hold sway, accompanied by considerable distress, anxiety and vulnerability. But these states can be temporary and in fact do not reflect the capacity and flexibility of the person in the overall and longer view.

We see other instances, however, where the loved person functioned to give the surviving person a sense of identity and self-worth, and a strong self-image. As soon as the loved person died the dormant incompetent self-image emerged as a prevailing state. What we see here is an apparent state of weakness and incompetence emerging after a loss, or after the news of that loss has registered and its meaning processed.

There are strong advocates of the view that this weakness is an hereditary weakness. Those who experience the weakness and helplessness seem more than ready to accept this view. It is convincing to them and it provides the valued excuse to avoid facing up to the new circumstances of life. They might say, "I have always known this is the kind of person I am" or "This thing runs right through the family ... it's hereditary."

Another view is that the helplessness is a result of

severe trauma and conflict. A sudden overload is placed on the person and they can no longer cope as they did. Their usual coping capacities are thrown into disarray; they begin to relive the past and retraverse their incompetence; they repeat patterns that they know will fail; no lesson is learned; the experience is painful and a kind of futile search for satisfaction and gratification continues. They hold onto the past to maintain a fragile sense of control and to avoid living in the new circumstances that would involve change, and pain. They resist facing the anxiety of disrupting the fantasy and the view of themselves that they want to maintain. In effect they fear a greater helplessness, rejection and loss of self-esteem, and thus their compulsive repetitive behavior is experienced as safer.

Many remain in this state. Grief counselors may erroneously believe that the person is in the process of positive grieving or working through their grief. The grieving person's reaction can be subtle and persuasive, and the situation is often so distressing that the counselor tends to identify with it, or with the person. In addition, a strong emotional arousal is readily provoked by particular tragedies.

Grieving people may be caught simultaneously in repetitive incompetence and in an incapacity to control their reactions or to repair the damage and so regain their sense of mastery and security. The process of recovery lies within their ways of thinking. They might talk about feeling their grief in the stomach, chest or legs, but it is primarily an activity that involves information and memory — and meanings that are attributed to that information and memory. From those meanings flows an emotional reaction which itself takes on a meaning that evokes further reactions: emotional and behavioral.

Robert, aged 27, was killed in a car accident while on vacation in another state. When his parents were given the news, they at first refused to believe it. They withdrew into themselves for several hours; they said they felt numb and dazed. They then began to confirm the information. He had been killed instantly. The image of the accident interacted frantically with the many memories that flashed into their minds. They began to feel shocked, empty, angry and helpless. They felt they should not be so angry and helpless and this led to confusion and guilt, panic and self-pity. They could not settle, they could not sleep. Robert's father began to vomit and the mother went to bed with all the symptoms of influenza.

While some might argue to accommodate these emotional, somatic and behavioral reactions as part of the grieving process, I argue that some measures of control are necessary to intercept these painful reactions. While some describe the parents' reaction as grief, I want to move immediately to relieve their pain and to specify strategies whereby that will be achieved.

If we can help people change their control functions or control strategies we would expect a change in their reactions and in their overall state. While many grief workers may be reluctant to acknowledge the urgency of this negotiated control, all workers in the field should recognize that control is an important goal. We are likely to hear "control" statements.

"He's got things under better control now."

"Everything was out of control; now she is coping better."

"It was difficult to get everything under control, but ultimately everyone recognized that some control was necessary."

Loss and death rarely stand on their own. They are likely to evoke memories, fantasies, images and apprehensions of earlier losses. Life begins with loss, ends with loss, and there are many losses in between. To some extent our attitude and beliefs about life and its losses, and our experiences with them, will influence the way we cope with a specific loss. We might look back and see how we coped with those earlier and sensitive experiences of separating from the parent, how the parent coped with loss, what our early models were. We might also reflect on the apprehension and experience of our mortality, aloneness and dependence, and our determination to leave a mark on the world. A new way of thinking is concerned with the way we integrate the experience and anxiety of early loss, the belief system we adopt in relation to the existential anxiety of our mortality, and the strategies we build up to cope with the specific contemporary loss and its aftermath reactions.

When an immediate stress is upon us, our early childhood experience of loss or our apprehension of our existential anxiety may seem irrelevant. We are sometimes surprised to find how our early experiences or our belief systems about ourselves can affect our ways of coping.

One woman in her late thirties had continuing difficulty dealing with the sense of loss in her life. She sought a solution in several relationships. They failed. When she realized how much her early infantile experiences affected her she began to adopt a different attitude. Discarded as an infant, she was adopted by parents who had problems — one became an alcoholic and the other was constantly angry and hostile. Rejected also by her peers at school, she felt driven to find success. She found it in her work and then demanded the same success in her personal relationships. But her earlier anxieties kept confusing and disrupting her chances.

Some people have difficulty coping with the anxiety of a current loss, because they have never learned how. Memories of past events, beliefs about themselves and attitudes toward the stress may mean they become so frightened and anxious that they cannot cope; their confidence and courage are eroded by the anticipatory anxiety of what "could" happen. Many have found that with a new way of thinking they can begin to rehearse and develop the appropriate behavior for this problem. This is called stress inoculation or self-instructional training. It involves gathering accurate information, developing possible plans of action, relaxing and while relaxed going through the plan of action in imagery. The person is asked to imagine the situation and they rehearse how they will cope. Sometimes it is necessary to build up a coping strategy in stages, with self-monitoring and relaxation, and gathering confidence. When the person has developed a coping strategy in imagery, they are encouraged to put it into action in the stressful situation itself.

When Michael told Joan he was going to leave her, she was very distressed though she had recognized for more than three years that the relationship had lost its positive energy and had become increasingly negative and hostile. Joan was not only losing Michael, she was losing what had been woven into their relationship over twenty years. She was losing status, face and pride. She said she would resign from her job as vice principal of the high school, because "I just could not bring myself to face the staff or the students ... they see me as someone in a very responsible position, and I cannot bear to think of them turning their heads and whispering about me." Fortunately, Joan sought help before she submitted her resignation.

Together, we were able to work out a plan of action — how she would cope with the actual separation from Michael and how she would cope with the shared belongings, the relatives and their friends. Her biggest anxiety was her perceived loss of face in the public arena of her work. She was able to change her perception by systematically identifying the beliefs, attitudes and cognitions she had of herself and of her public position — that is, that she should be seen to be invulnerable, without any shadows and almost bigger than human; that her resignation would somehow retain her sense of invulnerability and perfection; that "whispering" was necessarily harmful — it could be labeled differently to become part of the way her public audience would adapt to this new information.

Joan was very tense and tearful. She was encouraged to adopt a state of deep relaxation. In that trance state I asked her to imagine returning to the school — to identify in her images the people whose reactions she most feared. In her nonrelaxed state, she had spoken in terms of "the whole staff-room," "the school community" and "them." In her relaxed state, she identified five people whose reactions would disturb her. She began to see that the reaction of the school community — children and parents — had moved from being totally humiliating to temporarily embarrassing. In the relaxed state, I encouraged her to use several imagery techniques to see herself coping with her perceived difficulties. She rehearsed how she would cope. She imagined herself going through the situations that gave her the most anxiety. I then asked her to imagine how she would be in three weeks' time. I waited for her to describe the specific images of her future self-perception and self-competence.

After the relaxation period I then spoke with her about applying the techniques used in imagery to the actual situations in the school. She said she felt more confident. I stressed that the actual situation would have many aspects that would be different from the imagery we had used. But it would be possible for her to monitor her reactions to these situations, always reassured by the image she had of herself in three weeks' time.

6

Ruminations of the Mind

And David said: "While the child is yet alive, I fasted and wept, for I said; Who knows whether the Lord will be gracious to me and the child will live? But now that he is dead, why should I fast? Can I bring him back again? I shall go to him, but he will not return to me."

2 Samuel 12:22–23

… but I find
An image comforting the mind
And in my grief a strength renewed.

Alfred Tennyson

We know that grief and the distress of losing someone can provoke pain, aching and heaviness. But where do we feel those sensations? In the mind, in the body or in the way we experience our being in the world and our relating to the world? In our several ways we draw boundaries and say, "This is a mental pain" or "That is a physical pain," yet those boundaries may be ill-defined, illusory or fictitious. Because something happened in the past, we feel dreadful in the present, and wonder how we will face the future. Again, we use boundaries to break up our experience, yet we know only memories of the past, and those memories we experience in the present. Though we try to relive the past and get back in touch with it, at no point are we able to be directly aware of the past. There is no time but now, and this present is sandwiched in between what we label the past and what we anticipate will be the future.

The boundaries that we construct are our ways of understanding our experience, but they can be sources of persistent frustration and anxiety. We might hear people say, "I want to cross over the boundary and relive the past" or "Often I wish I could go back to a past moment — a particular 'then' which was once a 'now' like that, and another, and another." There is a strong resistance to revoke that desire to live in a previous moment. We want to dissolve the illusory boundary between the self as it was and the self as it is, between them and us. There is the necessity of living as separate entities and the awareness that nothing can be so separate and that all parts are held in a context. There is the reality of experienced alienation and loneliness and the yearning and drive for fusion and ecstasy.

Loss and death drop like a guillotine upon our experience and we collide with what seems to be an ultimate and non-negotiable imposed boundary. Human beings, probably since their earliest awareness of the mystery of their mortality, have tried to understand and destroy this boundary. We have been able to lengthen life, construct long-lasting memorials and symbols, devise theories of immortality, participate in religions of gods who offer the supreme prize of everlasting life and even a harp in heaven, but still we come to that boundary line and we die. No one knows what is beyond it.

When someone close to us dies, our mood changes, our behavior changes. We speak in a different tone of voice. We are no longer shouting and demanding, we are somber and slower. At these times, conventionally, we make contact with religious language, religious images and religious practices. We might even say this is a way to heal the spirit. For a few moments we might revert to that primitive apprehension that at death we are somehow saying our farewell to a spirit that is now migrating to another place. And lest that spirit assume power over us and visit some hazard upon us, we take care to be quiet and not speak ill of the dead. This is in contrast with an account R. D. Laing (1985) gave of his grandfather's funeral:

> ... my father was one of the purest spirits I have ever come across. Except for his father, I have never heard him hold anything against anyone. But I don't think he ever forgave his father for, as he believed, having done in his mother by turning her into "a nervous wreck". When my father and I were walking away from Old Pa's grave at his funeral, my father turned to me and said, "Now the bastard's dead". They were his only words (p. 77).

Though we are always contending with and clinging to our boundaries, we are nevertheless part of a kaleidoscopic flux, continuously changing patterns and textures, colors and contexts, but always in some observable and experiential relationship with the rest of the scene. It is this awareness that can become a major step toward the internal and mind reorganization that is necessary at times of loss and grief. Religious practices have always been used in this reorganization. Some forms of religion have been excessive in making claims for the role they should have at times of loss and grief. Society generally has not developed any other institution for this role, and has simply acceded to the practices of religion, with no critical examination as to whether this is the most effective, rational and helpful thing to do. In the organization of the inner mind that is necessary, we have to question whether the boundary lines emphasized by religion are conducive to this process — the boundary lines between this life and the next, between death and resurrection, God and man, good and evil.

In reorganizing our inner mind we draw new boundaries; we dissolve old boundaries; we touch the ultimate
metaphysical secret that we are part of a universe, a oneness, and that to realize the whole is to move toward
absorbing the pain of the parts.

A boundary line — even between the self and the not-
self — can shift. Ken Wilber (1979) wrote:

> [A boundary line] can be re-drawn. In a sense the person
> can re-map his soul and find in it territories he never
> thought possible, attainable, or even desirable (p. 5).

Our suffering and pain at times of loss and grief are
recognitions that we are in difficulty with our boundaries.
We wish the boundaries did not exist, that they could be
transcended or redrawn. We cannot live in the past. We
cannot be in two locations at the one time. We cannot
be alive and also among the dead. We cannot go to our
grave and be united with someone else who is in his or
her grave. What we can do is live in the present moment,
interpret our suffering in order to live it and also live
beyond it.

Our suffering becomes a mixture of the present distress
linked with memory and desire — a memory that constantly reactivates past images and a desire to cross
boundaries of the past and be reunited in the future. It is
so difficult to deal with this suffering that we become
stuck with it; it affects our whole style of living, our
behavior and our health and well-being.

The ruminations in our mind reflect how that suffering
is being experienced. It could be experienced differently
by helping the person redraw the boundaries. Of course
the resistance is very high and always understandable. But
grief's suffering calls for humane and urgent intervention;
it is not acceptable to say it has to take its own course.

Memories are difficult to recompose and render inactive. We know how often we forget important events and dates and faces; yet a distressing incident that occurred forty years ago can be recalled, apparently in minute detail. Traumatic memories, even if fragmentary, are not easily put to rest; when we begin to believe the memory is no longer so disturbing, it can suddenly reappear, and with greater force of disorganization and disruption. We function far below our potential and we experience long periods of sadness and helplessness. Part of us would indulge in magical thinking to wish the event had never occurred, that the past was obliterated, that the boundary was not there. Another part of us wishes we could forget and get on with living. And another knows we will never forget.

But — always — we are dealing with our distress, our own inner experience, our own mental processes. It is not an object called the past, but a subjective experience called the present. It is not some other body that needs to change. The one who is being most affected is ourselves. We cannot wipe out the memory but we know it is possible to change the memory's way of being a memory.

It is possible to change the way the memory sits in its context in our minds. It is possible to change the meaning of the memory and the language that we use to describe and interpret it. It is possible to create an inner environment and new circumstances, both internally and externally, whereby the memory will be less obtrusive and painful, more exposed to influences that will heal it and render it quiescent.

Folklore and common wisdom say that time will cure. When we look more carefully at the various processes involved, we see that more than time is involved. We begin to talk about the memory in different terms. We become part of new experiences. Some speak of the "expulsive power of a new affection." A new affection may be invested with such interest and excitement that the old affection that had been painful in its loss may be less important and obtrusive. A range of activities can collaborate to form an influence or an environment whereby the memory is experienced in a different way. Its priority in our hierarchy of concerns is changed and it becomes less likely to provoke maladaptive thinking and behavior.

We thus reorganize the memories and ruminations of the mind. I stumbled on this approach during an exploration of various meditative exercises. I later discovered that Milton Erickson had developed a format for hypnosis in psychotherapy which had readily identifiable applications to the management of traumatic memories and the pain experienced in loss and grief.

I had long been intrigued by the imagery that spontaneously occurred during states of relaxation and meditation. One segment of the autogenic relaxation training involves creation of imagery provoked by a word, a concept, a noise. At one place where I was teaching the method, I could not help but notice we were close to a railway station with trains stopping and starting every few minutes. The racket and noise were distractions and interruptions until we began to practice creating color images for the various noises: for the train as it was slowing down, and as it was gathering speed. I began to extend this into interpersonal relationships and conflict: choose the person who is being particularly frustrating. In a state of relaxation, recognize what part of your body that person is occupying; then practice changing the person to another part of the body, or rehearse ways to release the person from your body. As we practiced these exercises, it was clear that something was happening to the way we related to those people from that point onward. Was it not possible to do this with a person who had died or who had rejected us?

Around the same time I had read an article in a magazine on the theme of "finding your ally." The gist of the article, was that in a relaxed and meditative state some object — animal, insect, bird, person or moving entity — could appear spontaneously in imagery. This could be the kindly ally of your life. No matter what its form, it was important to pursue it and ask what it had to say to you. It sounded a little fantastic but I tried it with interesting results. I invited others to try it and they also reported positively and sometimes extensively on the experience. I then tried to create an ally to be helpful specifically in times of distress. This was not so successful and I realized that another course of action was indicated.

But the various explorations revealed that the mind had considerable freedom to maneuver and to create helpful images that convey messages and meanings of an unexpected and stimulating kind. We began to ask the ally: "Why am I suffering this? How can I change the degree of pain I am experiencing?" These simple questions asked to the image in this way quickly showed how the power of a memory could be changed by talking about it in more than one way at one time. It seemed that we were engaging different parts of the brain or different levels of consciousness. The words of the question were shaped to communicate with the dominant cerebral hemisphere, but the image, and the approach to the image, seemed to be more a concern of the nondominant hemisphere; not so much with the direct conscious mind but with a subliminal state of consciousness.

Our memories of a distressing event are not the actual event, though at times we function in ways that reflect that the memory is more stressful than the event itself was. We coped with the event and the tasks involved in the aftermath but the memory can tax us beyond the resources we perceive we have. In our memory distress we are not dealing with the actual and direct contact with the event and the world; we are dealing with what we believe it to be and what we construct it to be. We give it a particular meaning, we see it, we label it or build it into a context. We might distort the context, subtract from it, add to it and generalize to other situations, experiences and people. We can get stuck with that memory, its emotional loading, the language we use to describe it and its repetitive nature. The memory and the way we talk about it becomes a metaphorical statement about ourselves and our present life situation.

When people are grieving, the helpful friend or relative, or their counselor, may come to realize that the content of the memory and the retelling of it may not be relevant to the desired relief from the distressing memory. I have noted how often grieving people appear to believe that what actually happened back there is important, and that I would want to hear about it. What is important is what they are doing in their mind with that memory. Telling it over and over again may reflect more the person's outrage or helplessness than their doing the constructive work of bringing the memory of the trauma and their reaction to that trauma into a controlled and quiescent state.

"It does me good to talk it through again."

"I feel better when I have a good howl."

"It seems to build up and when I talk it over and go through it again, I can get back to work."

These comments and the suppositions that underlie them are very deceptive and mislead all parties into believing something beneficial is being done, when the benefits are far below what we have come to expect from a more deliberate process to reorganize memories and the meaning we give them.

When Beryl, aged 52, kept saying, "I feel so terrible," I knew she was talking about her grief pain provoked by the death of her husband ten days earlier.

I asked her: "*Where* do you feel terrible? When? How do you feel so terrible? And what is the feeling like?" I noted that she was not talking about her dead husband; she had said, "I feel," and so she was talking about herself. She described her state in the language of "I feel," and she let it stand on its own without any context.

As I carried through my exploration, I discovered that her feeling terrible was not so much related to the loss of her husband but to her guilt that she had been having a relationship with a man in addition to her husband for the previous six months. She feared that her children would somehow hear of her other relationship. No, she was not distressed by her husband's death. They had never had a satisfactory relationship. He had not been an involved father, and had not been a happy man; nor had he acted in any decisive way to improve that.

As I talked, her pain was being placed in a very different context from what I might have assumed. The language she used and the broader view she gave to her husband's death now allowed her to place a more accurate meaning on the inner sensations she was experiencing. She was also able to isolate or curtail this sensation rather than allowing it to flood her consciousness or generalize to her management and enjoyment of other relationships such as with her children. I noted that her feeling terrible was consequential to the way she had been thinking, to her beliefs and to the way she saw herself. Thus, although we might be induced to follow her feelings, we might be led away from this other language of thinking, believing and seeing.

Using Milton Erickson's mode of therapy, we might see in the grieving person's communication and description a surface structure and a deeper structure. When I visited the family of a young man who had been killed, I found the mother and father and two teenage daughters sitting together in the 23-year-old son's bedroom. He had been killed the previous day.

I asked, "What happened?"

The father replied, "He was hit by a car."

There was the surface structure and I could have left it there. But it was waiting like a tree laden with fruit seems to wait for someone to shake the bough. No one wanted to do that — you never know what might fall out of the tree. It happened at three in the morning. The son was walking back to his car with two of his friends. They had been drinking heavily. They did not see the car which others had said was traveling at high speed. Being "hit by a car" does not disclose that there was a driver in the car, that he did not stop and that all assumed he had also been drinking heavily. Here is the deeper structure, the unspoken context that was sitting behind the dazed faces and helpless grief of the family.

"How did your son die?"

"He was killed in the war."

"What happened to your wife?"

"She died of a heart attack."

"Where is your family?"

"They all perished in the Holocaust."

At one level, we are hearing all we need to know. At

another level we are hearing nothing of the meaning of the event or the context in which it has come to function within the person's thinking, feeling and behavior. The event and the memory can continue to be like constant baggage that the person carries everywhere, or it can be a baggage that the person knows is always there, but has been correctly stored in a back room of the house while the rest of the house has been furnished to live constructively for the present moment.

We necessarily must talk of these memories and the way they are managed in terms of metaphor — often because we have no other specific way of accurately describing them. Thus the distressing memory can be described as being a piece of furniture in the living room of the mind. This piece of furniture is large and no longer fits in the room comfortably; it is always there, obtruding and cumbersome. What would the room look like if we rearranged the furniture? If you called in three people in the quietness of the night to lift that cumbersome piece of furniture over into the corner? If you then decorate the corner so that that furniture began to blend more with the room? If you went out and bought furniture that would be useful and comfortable for your current needs?

By metaphor and image we have regained a sense of control over a distressing event, we have acknowledged the presence of the memory; we have not tried to eradicate it. We have simply asked what things would look like if we could retain the memory so that it would be there in a different way of being there from what it was before. We have raised the possibility of changing the place, the context, the significance and the meaning of the memory. We have restructured the memory, its context and the environment. Suppose, then, that this process could be done in a form of inner-mind reorganization while the relevant parts of the grieving person's consciousness were amenable, and the memory itself was accessible.

This happened with excellent effect with one of my own troublesome memories that was frequently reactivated and in various relationships was repetitively though unintentionally reinforced. The content of the memory was not important or relevant. Its meaning and the significance I gave it were. The actual event occurred years earlier. I had acted in a way that in hindsight I wished I had not. That action had a devastating effect on the people concerned, though for a time I felt I had done the right thing and that I had benefited.

Gradually I realized the size and significance of my misjudgment. Both the memory of what I had done and the results of my misjudgment grew in their burden and generalized into other contexts. There was a strong persistent magical wish to retrieve the whole situation, to recross boundaries of time, space, context and people, and do it all over again, but correctly. In many different ways and on several occasions I attempted to do that but it was impossible.

If you throw one stone into the pool it sends out its ripples and vibrations in so many ways that the ecology of the pool is uniquely disturbed by that stone. Though you take the same stone and throw it in the same spot, the disturbance caused in the pool will be different and it will be impossible to trace it or stop it.

So with the structure of our judgments and decisions: so many things happen because of that decision that you cannot start over again — new boundaries have been drawn, new people have become part of those changed contexts. The pool once disturbed will resume its calm state, but changed in a myriad of ways.

I noticed the language I was using about my memory: I said often,

"I wish I could go back and do it all over again."

"I see now that I could have taken a different road."

"I walked away when I should have held my ground."

"I was in too much of a hurry."

Unlike the woman who described her memory as "very sad, very heavy and very flattening" (that is, in terms of weight and somatics) my description was in linear, directional and speed terms. That was the language that gave it its loading, and it was the language that persistently reflected the various contexts in which I saw myself in relation to that memory and the way it affected the other decisions and directions of my life.

One day, in a quiet, relaxed time and place, and at least twenty years after the actual event, I thought I would ask "my ally" what I might do about this memory that was now enclosed by several impossible boundaries. When at length all hurry had gone from me, and I was passively relaxed, I heard my ally say: "Be patient and wait."

With some impatience and with all the conscious recognition that nothing could change anything in relation to that memory, I waited. Needless to say, nothing happened. I relaxed more passively.

At once I saw I was in a very old boardinghouse. Each morning as I went to work I came down the stairs into the entrance hall where there was a mirror and a coatrack on one side of the hall and a blurred and shadowy picture in an old frame on the other side of the hall. I looked at the picture as I had done apparently every morning. But on this day something told me it was time to put that tarnished and now useless picture in the attic. I forthwith did so. As I walked down the stairs I reflected with a sadness barely tinged with relief that I would not have to look at the picture again — unless I made the specific trip to the attic to see it.

From now on it would be my decision whether I would see it, rather than it always being available to me every time I walked in and out the front door. In this way, my memory took on a completely new context, meaning and accessibility. I was able to decide about myself and my direction in relation to the memory, and the boundary lines that I had drawn and now redrawn.

In helping people with their inner-mind reorganization I ask them to be passively relaxed and gently allow themselves to enter a quiet, reflective trance state. On the one hand they will concentrate on each word I use, but on the other hand I will choose words, language and imagery that will slip under their rational evaluating consciousness to the subliminal levels of consciousness. Having already listened carefully to the language the grieving person is using about their grief, I will begin to use words, language and images relevant to the description, context and meaning they have given their loss and their memory of that distressing event. I slow down the words and change the tone of voice, and using several images and themes, I begin to create a freedom to maneuver. As I pace the language and access the distressing memories, I look for the possibility of changing the way of perceiving, describing and experiencing the pain; I look for ways to rearrange the internal furniture, the context and the meanings that are given to the context.

I make analogical shifts as I talk to one part of awareness but place strengthening messages and images in that other subliminal part of awareness. To counter the distortions and deletions that have been part of this maladaptive memory and meaning, I take the language of their anxiety and pain and lay it closely alongside the symbols and images of relaxation and strength. Alongside their perception of themselves clinging to their memory, I might place before them the image of a bird flying away from a tree. The bird flies on. The tree has fulfilled a valued function and then let the bird go without regret or sadness. A person may wander through the remains and ruins of a building, over the place of activity now deserted except for the cold wind. If we listen the wind may carry a message to the ruins to which to this point the ruins have been oblivious. Now the message comes through. Or it may be the wind has a message to the grieving person — "Look at the grass that grows through the concrete."

One elderly man said of his wife: "It was terrible to see her suffering like that. It was such a painful way to go ... just terrible."

I waited for the silence and then I said very slowly: "It was painful for her to go, and it was painful the longer she stayed. Perhaps she knew she couldn't stay, but she hung on in pain until you could let her go ..." In actuality, she had already gone, but now he was in pain as he kept recalling her pain. My words to him immediately changed the meaning of what he was doing in the present — holding onto her. By letting go, she and he, in effect, were released from their pain.

Inner-mind reorganization may involve the use of *embedded questions*, *embedded conversation* and *embedded commands* in my words to the grieving people.

"Your memory of your daughter ... it's as if you have put her in a particular frame, labeled it and hung it on the wall. Every day you read that label. Every day you feel the pain. What would happen if we changed the frame? What would happen if we put your daughter in a new and quite different frame? What would happen if we put another label on the frame? ... Instead of labeling it 'pain I cannot forget,' could we label it 'courage and inspiration' or 'a small part of a larger whole'?"

I have here embedded questions and conversation with ample freedom for the person to explore the changes that come from these different possibilities. We raise questions, suggest rearranging their inner world. We can walk around the memory, give it a different meaning, speak to it a message that could change its impact and restructure its place in the person's way of being and his way of meeting the world.

A command can also be embedded. This can take several forms.

"Every time you think of your daughter you will remember her courage and inspiration. Whenever you do this quiet reflection you will say quietly, 'I see myself as part of a larger whole, and it surrounds me with good and positive influences.'

"After you have waited and taken good time to let a little healing come to your whole being, you wait until you feel that you have reached a point of completion, then you come out of your reflective state and say, 'I am ready to go on.'"

When a memory is distressing, the grieving person senses the anxiety and nonhealing toxic nature of their inner experience and inner environment. They also recognize that their interaction with the outer world is not relaxed or hospitable. With relaxation and restructuring, they begin to create an inner world that is conducive to healing and quiescence. With different breathing and relaxation the interaction with the outer world also becomes more receptive and collaborative in the healing process.

A 34-year-old woman remained distressed for five months. She had been very attached to her father. One weekend he had visited her and her family. As he was leaving her house on the Sunday evening, he took his coat from her and immediately collapsed and died. She said, "I cannot get out of my mind the sad and helpless look on his face at the moment he collapsed. I have been depressed ever since it happened. He had not been ill. There had not been a single sign that he was going to die. It was such a terrible shock, but above all it was the look on his face."

I asked her what she thought the look was trying to communicate. After some thought, she said it looked as if he suddenly knew a screen had dropped and there was nothing more he could say or do. "It was just so sad, so helpless."

I asked her to be relaxed in a passive, reflective trance state. I asked her to replace the event of the memory in its original context: her father taking leave from the door, then collapsing at her feet. I asked her to go on from there.

"Yes," she said, "when we saw he was gone, my husband and I lifted him onto the couch in the living room. We took the children out of the room and closed the door. And we called the ambulance. They came, just looked at him and took him away. I was so upset I couldn't leave the bedroom." She began to cry.

I told her to breathe strongly; to take time; to prepare herself for something that would now change the distress and pain within her. Very slowly I suggested that we go back to the image of her father on the couch in the living room prior to the ambulance arriving. In effect, as she and her husband had closed the door, she had drawn a boundary around her father and her memory of her father. Now I suggested it might be possible for her to open that boundary again for a few minutes and make a new contact with her memory of events on that night.

"Wouldn't it be interesting," I said, "if you could cross over all the boundaries that have now been drawn, and while you are awaiting the ambulance, you quietly slip into the room where your father is lying? No one sees you. You are quite alone. Remember, you thought that the look on his face may have been his attempt to say something? But now he does not speak. He is waiting for you. You go behind the couch on which he is now peacefully lying. And you bend over him. Perhaps you would now say something to him that would be your most important word to him before he finally goes. Perhaps you could say to him, 'I'm so pleased you died here and not on your own ... I'm so pleased you died here and not as you were driving home ... I'm so pleased you were with me and all of us in the moments before you died ...'"

She cried. I then gently gave the command that she should give him the message she would most like to give him. "Look carefully at him so that you can see the message is right. Check carefully to see the message is right. Then say good-bye. Take time until you feel it is complete and what you have done is good ... and you feel right about it. Then you come and sit with me and talk with me about what you have done."

She later said the whole experience had made the event and the memory so different that she was confident she could cope with it. In the process, we had made contact with her distressing memory, we restructured it, placed it in a different context, introduced a new part to it and took time to allow the inner environment to begin to contribute to the healing. We had also taken time to help her realise that she could once again assume control over her life and be enlarged by her father's death rather than be hurt and diminished by it.

In this inner-mind restructuring we sometimes find that one part of the memory or some part of the person's experience will not allow healing to take place. There is a part blocking or resisting, or there is a part that is missing or out of place. Sometimes it seems that one part has become the provocation of the recurring state of distress but it has forgotten or it does not know why it is doing it. In the reflective state we make contact with this part to see what it is doing and would like to do.

One man said, "I'm way out in the middle of a lake in a boat. I've just thrown something into the lake. I don't know what it was, but it has sunk to the bottom. I'm sitting there looking and feeling very miserable."

I asked him, "What would happen if we could get into communication with what you threw overboard? What would you say to it ... what is it saying to you?"

He said, "It says you are going to feel pretty bad now that you've thrown me out."

I asked, "Could you ask it to come back ... will it come?"

There was a long pause and then he said awkwardly, "Yes, it's coming back but it says it has found something at the bottom of the lake, and it wants to bring that back too. It says it should help me."

I asked, "Are you going to take it on board?"

"You bet," he said.

There are times when in this imagery the person can and will create a new part that is as good as the part that has been making them so miserable. The person can actually say, "I want a part that will change my loneliness ..." or "I want a part that will nicely transform my anger and frustration ..."

What would happen if they could have that part? Would the other parts accept it? How would they behave?

We might then follow through a sequence of events of their feeling and behaving differently with the new part acceptably in place. It is important to proceed slowly, for the person to take time to explore the image, so that they can become aware of what they would need to know or do, to be able to build a new part into their experience that could do what was needing to be done for rapid healing in each moment it was needed. In effect, the person explores stepping inside the fantasy and having the experience of actually doing it.

At first, this process may appear too unrealistic. It is, however, simply a more directional and planned way of doing what all therapy attempts to do as it builds new strengths, or turns to different parts to heal wounds, and organize or integrate past events into a constructive adaptation and growth in the present.

7
Focusing of the Mind

I know that faith is like a root
That's tough, inert, and old;
Yet it can send up its green shoot
And flower against the cold.

I know there is a grace that flows
When all the springs run dry.
It wells up to renew the rose
And lifts the cedars high.

James McAuley

People who have experienced a severe loss find that their mind will frequently be out of control. Thoughts of the lost person or object flood into the mind and there are thoughts of self-blame and blaming of others, and ruminations on the emptiness and purposelessness of life. There is a loss of the capacity to concentrate on tasks and an easy distractability and a readiness to persist in destructive and depressive interpretations of events and life generally.

People are usually affected by four closely associated losses — loss of control over their thoughts, loss of their resistance capacities, loss of the sense of meaning and purpose, and loss of the sense of self-worth and self-efficacy. Many say that prior to the trauma they had not at any time experienced any difficulty with mind control, but the trauma itself seemed to shatter their confidence and make them vulnerable to the invasion of negative thoughts, anxieties and fears.

Helpers are likely to affirm that this is the nature and power of the trauma, and these are the expected reactions. Once again, there is a readiness to accept the pathology of the situation, express sympathy and support, and provide reassurance that "things will come right" eventually.

The laziness of grief and the collusion in that laziness by the helpers can mean that people may remain for too long in this state. We overlook that most people have never been taught how to control and focus the mind, especially after an emotional disruption and disturbance. There is the readiness to believe that anxious worrying is somehow normal because that is how most people tend to behave.

It is possible to learn mind or consciousness focusing; to learn how to reorganize resistance and to restore lost confidence, even in the face of external attack or in spite of persistent self-sabotage.

Mind control and consciousness focusing involve:

1   Bringing to full consciousness and recognition all aspects of the worrying and preoccupation, to identify what it is that a person is worrying about or hanging onto
2   Separating the basic anxiety from the secondary emotions that readily cling to it and give it added significance, pressure and apparent insatiability
3   Recognizing how the basic anxiety rapidly fuses with secondary emotions to persuade people that they are a failure, "a dead loss," unworthy, and that life has no meaning.

Once this fusion is recognized, action must be repeatedly taken to separate these issues and concerns, and to keep the pursuit of the meaning of life apart from traumas that require specific coping skills. When the doctor has a poisoned foot, he does not begin to question the meaning of life because of that; he adopts the appropriate procedure to deal with the poisoned foot. When the same doctor loses a wife or a patient, that only becomes a matter to involve the meaning of life insofar as he interprets it that way. But he still has to discover the appropriate procedure to deal with his trauma.

The basic anxiety having been identified, it then becomes the full focus of attention. It is important to concentrate on it fully and exhaustively, to examine the assumptions and beliefs that are associated with it and to identify the inner dialogue that goes on about it. Sometimes it is necessary to grieve out the emotional residues and to transform the object of attachment into an object of increasing detachment. The persistent preoccupation with and addiction to the worry generally reflects that the worry has come to represent and symbolize something more than its own basic content. The worry can become both metaphor and parable and acquire an emotional loading and import which also needs to be designated and evaluated for its appropriateness and its way of being contained or expressed.

The restless and agitated scanning of the mind and thought processes can be accepted as part of the reaction of loss or it can be seen as a phenomenon that can be anticipated, intercepted and controlled. A person soon comes to recognize the people, events and thoughts that readily become triggers to set off the scanning and the worrying. If these can be recognized early enough, avoidance and evasion will become considered possibilities, or if they trigger off the distress before prevention can be put into effect, then the course of the distress can be monitored and, eventually, intercepted with skill and satisfaction.

People can begin the process of retraining their minds for short-term focusing on positive mood-enhancing events and experiences. As this skill is being developed, rewards and satisfying feelings can enhance the experience and encourage further exploration and involvement in the training. Sometimes an elementary rehearsal of these skills is required as with the building of courage training. (See Macnab, 1985.) Each fear requires identification and rehearsal to deal with it. Models for the behavior can be helpful, as can be the encouragement of a support group.

Resistance becomes a valuable attribute, especially when a person can feel highly vulnerable, and easily swept back into negative and distressing thinking. Resistance resources may be drawn from four areas:

1 *Within the self* — attitudes, mood control, perceived self-management and self-efficacy, organization of past experiences, imagination management, freedom from irrational and neurotic behavior, freedom from an oppressive or restricting conscience, a capacity to enjoy life and develop a positive sense of well-being within oneself
2 *Other people* — significant nurturing relationships, audiences that are encouraging and enhancing, imagined and fantasied audiences that are facilitative and inspirational, supportive influences and groups
3 *Confirmatory experiences* — derived from people who are, or have been, significant and positive models and superiors; religious and spiritual influences; the capacity to enter into a regular positive self-review; a conception of life that is stable but sufficiently flexible

to be responsive to the transitions and traumas and the necessary losses

4 *Physical considerations* — health and fitness, financial resources, other resources such as status, domestic and work arrangements; distractions and compensations; art, music, poetry and pets that lift, encourage and transform; powerful passions, pursuits and goals.

A number of strategies can become part of our resistance resources — relaxation techniques; learning how new perspectives can change the management of stresses; the capacity to distinguish between coping that is focused on the identified problem, and the coping necessary to deal with the emotions with which the problems are associated or with which they become freighted. Resistance resources involve the development of the capacity to listen to and control the inner voice, the voice of belief, attitude, assumption and fear. Just as images can sabotage the best of efforts, so images can be used to create a positive coping, an expectancy about oneself and the future. Whereas the focus of worry can be so restlessly internal, people can train themselves to externalize the worry, to convert it into a problem or object that can be placed outside the self, rather than left to war inside the self. The power of former bonds can be examined, and using imagery, self-talk and courage rehearsal, the power of these bonds can be reduced and finally broken.

A great deal depends on the person's perception of their self-worth, self-confidence and self-efficacy, where they see self-worth coming from, and upon what they see it depends.

In the task of consciousness refocusing, we usually find that there is a need to rebuild self-skills and reconstruct self-worth. People have had great difficulty coping with loss and grief because neither they nor anyone else recognized that their sense of self-worth and self-efficacy called for careful review and some positive reconstruction. Too often it is simply accepted that people feel "low" after a loss, and with generalized sympathy and support, patience and reassurance, "it will all come right." I propose a much more humane approach to this anguish and pain of low self-worth.

At the outset it is helpful to distinguish the various expressions of the low sense of self, for this usually leads to specific strategies of restoration. Low sense of self may be experienced as:

1 A total loss of everything important
2 An abandonment by one person
3 Loss of purpose in job and status while significant relationships are stable
4 A sense of inner collapse without identifiable supportive resources
5 The experience of repetitive self-blame and self-sabotage
6 Helplessness and depression
7 Undeveloped and unstable resources
8 A generalized disorganization that is interpreted as loss of self-confidence
9 Identified low self-esteem
10 Unidentified low self-esteem
11 Misidentified low self-confidence, with inner rage and strength being frustrated
12 Damage to the self through surgery, stroke, sickness, accident
13 Low self- and social skills.

Our objective is to help the person move toward a more

positive functioning and feeling, and toward perceiving and experiencing themselves moving toward that objective. They will recover the sense of who they are, what they are going to do, where they are going to direct their lives, and from what sources they will gain motivation and the sense of well-being. Strategies that will be relevant will focus on:

1 Freeing the person's sense of self from previous experiences and traumas
2 Freeing the person from inner constriction, sabotage, punitive fantasies, wishes and demands
3 Re-establishing the context of their current lives and rehearsing their autonomy within it
4 Developing a philosophy of human identity, behavior, values and expectations, and seeing their own growth within it
5 Enlisting previous history, coping strategies and models in the process of restoration and growth
6 Identifying experiences and people who will be facilitative and supportive and those who are destructive; and rehearsing attitudes and determination regarding them both
7 Entering into an inner dialogue with events, experiences, fantasies and images that block growth, and those that pull toward growth, fulfillment and ecstasy
8 Pursuing images, symbols and practices that engender healing, confidence and self-worth.

The following example shows how a person became preoccupied with guilt — and what he could have done, and how things might have been different if he had followed these steps. When he first presented his problem, he said he was stuck: "I just can't get over it and I can't get on with life!" He found some effective distraction while he was at work, but as soon as he returned home he was immediately reminded of his plight and his thoughts were once again out of control. His one significant relationship which had considerable potential was plundered nightly by his ruminations. Although his self-esteem and self-efficacy appeared to be in good shape, in fact he was fragmented — trying to place himself in two relationships: one with his companion and one with his dead wife. He said the whole event had "shattered" him and his restoration depended on getting him "together" again.

The dilemma presented below is given as a small segment of this overall process. It was written immediately after one session with him, as a summary of the therapy that had taken place during that session.

Your dilemma

"I feel guilty that I did not take Janet back. We had parted on her demand. She had entered a relationship with another man. I was devastated. I pleaded with her to return. She refused. Later, when her relationship ended, and her circumstances and attitudes changed, she insisted on coming back to me. We tried it and it was disastrous. It was no good and we parted. But she kept up her plea to return. Ultimately, she took her life on a night after I had refused to have her back.

Response

There are two phases to consider: when Janet was alive and after her death. When Janet was alive, she pleaded to come back. You rejected this.

1   You were already involved in a satisfying and success-
     ful relationship with Catherine.
2   You were conscious of the fact that you had withdrawn
     your love from Janet, and now loved Catherine.
3   The strong bond you once had and valued with Janet
     had been severed.
4   You knew that the marriage had broken down and
     could not be resumed.
5   You discovered a freedom and personal enhancement
     in your relationship with Catherine that you had not
     known with Janet.
6   This did not mean you ceased caring about and for
     Janet. She had been a significant part of your life over
     a long period and she was the mother of your four
     children. You cared but Janet tried to turn this caring
     back into a bonded relationship which you no longer
     wanted or could affirm.

After Janet's death, you became distressed by the
thought that had you taken her back when she asked, she
would not have destroyed herself. Now, after her death,
it is *as if* she is trying to get you to come back to her. It is
as if she is trying to curtail your enjoyment and your ongoing life. You will recognize that it is not actually Janet
doing this to you ...

1   The memory of Janet has become a powerful force, a
     hook.
2   But the memory is your own *mind* process.
3   You are attributing power to her image that she did
     not have while she was alive.
4   You have said, in the context of your relationship with
     Catherine, how boring your marriage had become.
5   But you continue to let Janet or her image in your

mind tyrannize and punish you and preclude you from the future. But Janet is now something inside yourself. It is necessary for you to practice putting that outside yourself, and seeing it for what it is.

6   Prior to meeting Catherine you had made several strong offers to Janet to return. Later you continued to do so, knowing the "real chemistry" was with you and Catherine. It is important to accept this as your own statement, and your own reality.

Something to practice

You need some relevant imagery to help you more effectively sever yourself from the memory of Janet:

1   Janet is like a book. The book is complete. Place it on the shelf.
2   We notice you keep going back to look again at the book. Thus, it is important to place the book in the attic where only rarely will you be in a situation where it will be seen and touched.
3   It seems that one manifestation of the book is your house and its furnishings. In order to move away from the memories of Janet adequately, you may need to sell this house *or* develop different attitudes toward it.
4   It is important to recognize that along with this process, some new doors have been opened to you. Without your seeking it, your employer has offered you a promotion. Without demanding it, Catherine is offering you a different relationship. Without your contriving, other doorways, which raise new questions about your ongoing career, are opening to you. All of these need to be explored. They now can be

explored, whereas previously you were heavily involved in other preoccupations. You can now bring your thinking to consider each of these matters, whereas previously you were entangled in an acute anguish which kept you from the freedom that you now can experience and explore.

8

Sorting Out Our Body Reactions

Health is accorded a positive value in Western Society, yet paradoxically many persons choose illness as a way of life.

Charles Ford

This is my body which is broken for you.

Jesus of Nazareth

From our common experience, we know how a tense and frustrating encounter with someone can leave us with a splitting headache. After witnessing a distressing incident we can feel faint and ill. Anxiety and a sense of powerlessness can drive us to overeat and become overweight. Anger and fear affect our pulse rate and blood pressure, and worry plays a part in discomfort of our indigestion and the pain of our gastric ulcers. What we see, hear and feel can affect our body reactions, from acute and temporary pain, through to prolonged conditions that disturb our relationships, our sense of well-being, and come to be a threat to life itself.

Before the middle of the seventeenth century, the body and mind were accepted as vital to a person's well-being, and the mind and emotions were seen to play an important part in illness, recovery and health. About the middle of the seventeenth century, and particularly with the philosophy of Descartes, the mind was split off from

119

the body. The mind and soul were dissociated from biological functions, and this set the scene for more than two centuries. Scientific medicine became primarily concerned with the body; matters of mind and soul were regarded as philosophy (and, later, psychology). When people developed illnesses and conditions for which there was no organic or physical origin, they were told "It's in your mind!" or "Your imagination has got the better of you!" The person was made to feel stupid, inferior and ineffective, that they had become a helpless victim of their imagination which was out of control. The onus was put on the person to "pull themselves together," and curtail their imagination.

It did not occur to doctors and others who held such contempt for the imagination that they were revealing their own ineffectiveness in understanding the power of the mind and imagination. If mind and imagination had such an influence, then it was the doctor's task to "treat" that imagination, curtail its influence and teach the person how it could be one of their most positive resources for health and well-being. But this was not done. A wide range of physical conditions can develop and which seem to be intertwined with mind, imagination and emotions. Some people become angry that this should mean their symptoms and sicknesses are not real. Such has been the division of body and mind that when the body cries out for attention, that is acceptable, but when the mind and soul cry out for help, there is a strong apprehension that there is something bogus about that.

In many people's lives, it is not a matter of making an either–or distinction between body and mind difficulties — both are involved. One woman had been the victim of several car crashes; in each it was proved beyond doubt that she had played no faulty part in these crashes, except being there at the wrong time. She had injuries to her back and neck which gave her prolonged and difficult pain. Whenever she went driving, she was excessively vigilant and anxious. This provoked spasms of tension and fear which induced a different range of symptoms — mouth pain, headaches and high blood pressure. Thus she had three realities to deal with: the actual injuries at the time of the crashes, the aftermath pain and the psychological or mind states which were tied to her past experiences but were more particularly evoked by the anticipation of stressors (that is, stressors which had not yet occurred). She had lost her sense of security and stable expectation, and events which would be minor to most people became events of major threat to her.

Our losses gather so many feelings around them — some of them are recognized, some concealed — that we have come to expect some body reactions. We are still puzzled by how this occurs. Why do feelings become translated into body reactions? Why these particular reactions? Why these particular body organs? We are sometimes shocked by the extent of such body reactions which can affect the nervous system, the gastrointestinal system, the reproductive–urino–genital system and the vascular and respiratory systems.

We have probably noticed how quickly people have caught a cold after moving from one job to another, or after a death in the extended family. Others report gastric distress, heightened blood pressure and bowel problems. Many people search for some cause of their chronic facial pain or the debilitating back pain. They may find that their pain is somehow linked with their change of life-style or the bereavement they have experienced. The pain may become a symbol and metaphor of the person's current situation, or an unconscious defense against the anxiety of facing the new reality of their future. Bereaved people and those who have lost their goals or direction or raison d'être may find they are visiting their doctor or seeking consolation and support more frequently and extensively than their nonbereaved counterparts. Their symptoms may be obviously and demonstrably physical, like chest pains, heart palpitations, sleeplessness, diarrhrea, abdominal pain, vomiting, nausea and various respiratory difficulties. Other symptoms may be more subjective and not have a demonstrable origin, but may be just as distressing — oral pain, dizziness, blurred vision, loss of memory, loss of sexual desire, loss of voice. The doctor, through training and practice, may focus on the physical problem, on the assumption that the physical factors have exclusive priority. The ensuing process can be time-consuming and time-wasting. It can involve a vast overuse of medical and health services as people move from one diagnostic center to another, one treatment agency to another. Inevitably the costs are high. Charles Ford (1983) wrote of the situation:

> At the present time the annual costs for medical care exceed $200 billion (US Bureau of the Census, 1980). If one were to assume that 10% of all medical care (not including psychiatric treatment) is provided to persons with no organic disease, then the total cost would be $20 billion per annum. This figure does not even include disability payments or time lost from work. Somatization is a large industry! (p. 3).

Many body conditions persist, not only because their connections are not identified, but because of misplaced reassurances, overprotectiveness and unwitting reinforcement by the helping professions. People sometimes say, "It takes a long time to get over something like that" or

"You never get over things like that." Helpers can be so entangled in their own "homespun" philosophy, their own losses or their overidentification with other people's losses, that a kind of collusion takes place and the person's pain is given a permission to persist.

Some of our inner wounds are invisible. We do not see them; we may have denied that we were wounded; we went on as if nothing had happened. But these invisible wounds can gradually do their damage. Body symptoms appear and we may not make any connection with the earlier inner wounds. The body symptoms may become a distraction or a way of detaching ourselves from our inner pain, or they may become a symbol of our loss and our need. A grief reaction can lay dormant for months or years. At length it may emerge in a serious body illness and sometimes as a symbol of the inner alienation and pain that have been held under control for so long, and yet the connection may be missed. The conditions may be treated but the underlying pain may go unrecognized.

Connections may be missed in other ways. One man had an uncomfortable condition for forty years, received extensive and sophisticated treatment without its link with an earlier painful loss ever being recognized. Irritable bowel syndrome, ulcers, angina, arthritis, respiratory conditions, alcoholism and cancer may become accepted as "what we have" — a way of life — without any connection with a past loss or trauma being explored. We are all caught up in the vulnerability of our humanity. Many in the helping professions who have not settled their own losses or who are driven by their fear of loss may evade or discount the possible influences of other people's losses. It needs to be emphasized that losses here embrace the early losses of significant intimacy, the loss of people, the loss of status, the loss of dignity, the loss of the dream of who I want to be and who I want others to perceive me to be. These losses and anxieties of losses have worried and driven people over many generations.

One man knew he had been upset by the loss of his promotion and the loss of the status that the new position would have brought him. He also lost the fantasy he had begun to build up of himself and his position in his world view. At the time of his loss he repeatedly went over all the things he could have done. He sought some solace from others. The hurt was unabated. Eventually he told himself it was not the end of the world.

Another career path opened and he pursued it successfully. Eight years later he developed an abdominal cancer which was surgically removed. His anxiety was aroused and he sought psychotherapy to explore if there were destructive attitudes involved in his cancer and if there was some action that could be taken to prevent any further cancers. It was not long before he began to reflect on the earlier loss of promotion: "It was an awful kick in the guts," he said. Although his cancer had been removed, nothing had been done to remove the concealed anger and disappointment, the loss of self-image and the loss of pride. "I never really got over that and although nobody would ever have known it, my own inner view of myself changed."

With some of our loss experiences, we know we have been wounded. We might openly recognize that, and talk about it; yet without our being aware of it, these recognized wounds may make their own connections in the mind, and later we may come to realize what these connections were and how they came to trigger diffuse or specific body reactions.

How does a person come to convert their sense of loss and their emotional conflict and pain into body symptoms? There are no simple or universal answers to this question. Specific individuals are rarely consistent enough to make generalizations or predictions about how they will respond to such stresses in their life. Many schools of thought have advanced their ideas as to why and how such body reactions occur and these ideas are part of a debate that will necessarily continue.

Lack of Information

People lack information. They do not know what to do with their feelings or how to control them constructively. At times they are not aware of what their feelings are. They may recognize that an event has distressed or troubled them. They have a need to deal with the event and the distress. If body reactions also become mixed with both of these, they have an additional need to do something about these body reactions. They may also have a need to remain aloof and self-reliant, however unsure they may be about what to do with all of these feelings that seem to clamor for expression. They have probably never been taught to identify their feelings nor to know whether and how these feelings should be discharged or controlled. They function below their general effectiveness, their relationships become strained and they become low on productivity, spontaneity and good company. A specific body organ or the body generally becomes a way of signaling this diffuse distress.

These people may seek various kinds of help for their conditions and this process may also reflect how greatly they need sound information and advice, as well as awareness and insight.

Previous Experiences

People are affected by their earliest experiences of closeness and separation, discovery and loss, awareness and alienation, anticipation and disillusionment. These experiences may be single traumatic events or they become repetitively interwoven with the nature of early relationships. Those relationships and environments affect our way of coping with our losses and can set the stage for the way we cope with losses throughout the life span.

From earliest days, body reactions are closely connected with emotional reactions — frustration may be reflected in constipation; anxiety and tension in colic and vomiting of food; fear and anger through breathing difficulties. Early environments affect the way body symptoms become vehicles of emotional states, how they are disclosed and concealed, described and interpreted, intercepted and treated.

Very early in life, people discover the power of a body state, whether it is accepted, given attention, reinforced, or whether it is discounted, ignored, punished. They learn whether feelings can be expressed or whether it is better to conceal those feelings somehow, and develop a body symptom. This can bring special treatment, create a different environment which in time will affect their ongoing thinking, feeling and behavior. The parent–child environment can be so confusing, with love and fear in flux, with an ambience of expectation and inescapability, that a body symptom can be a valued distraction, a way of detachment, a solace, a way of appeasing an indescribable anxiety. Some people find ways of getting on with life, and the childhood event diminishes in its significance and power. Others find that the anxiety persists, and from time to time, it exerts a disturbing impact on their lives. Body symptoms may develop. Instead of allaying anxiety, they may create further anxiety.

Conditioning Processes

A conditioning process can play a part in body reactions. A particular body reaction becomes associated with an emotional state, with a person, with an event, a memory or a date. The body reaction may disappear, but can reappear should the original stimulus, or a symbol of it, recur.

Such reactions are common on anniversaries. Because of a sensitivity about an anniversary, some people may experience body reactions. It is also a well-known phenomenon that the type of illness or the date of death may have a connection with the meaning given to an anniversary. Anniversary reactions include physical conditions, such as colitis, asthma or cardiac arrest; psychological disorders like anxiety and depression; or behavioral problems like overeating, alcohol and substance abuse, erratic driving on the roads and financial excesses.

Other forms of conditioning can take place. A person may find that body illnesses attract sympathy and concern. Their role as a sick person permits them to be perceived and treated differently. They may be released from their normal responsibilities and be absolved from any blame for their condition. If we imagine the person being able to admit openly that their problem was one of not being able to get over the loss of their 20-year-old daughter who left home a year ago, they may fear that others would be unsympathetic and put the onus directly on them to hurry up and make the adjustment. But if they develop a physical condition of severe migraines or of being overweight and constantly tired, they are largely — if not totally — excused from a personal responsibility for their condition or its relief.

People are generally sympathetic and supportive and, in the early stages at least, they show a willingness to be helpful. As the condition persists or worsens, the reactions of others may change to anxiety, frustration, anger and despair. In some instances the person with symptoms will be reminded of the obligation to seek competent help, to abandon the sick role as quickly as possible and to cooperate fully with all attempts to help them recover. If, however, the provocation of the condition was a distressing loss (which may have touched anxieties of earlier, perhaps sensitive, childhood losses) then the alienation they experience, and the anger and demands of current relationships, may worsen their sense of loneliness and distress and the bodily symptoms. They may also feel reinforced in their belief that their repetitive traumas justify their body reactions, and they themselves feel vindicated.

Body Symptoms and Sicknesses

Body symptoms and sicknesses are often closely linked to actual and perceived vulnerabilities. A person may view their episode of influenza as part of the infection sweeping through the community and may not recognize that a recent loss or trauma has affected their immune system, making them more vulnerable to infection. Our knowledge of how and why the immune system breaks down is limited but there is growing evidence to indicate that the immune system operates through the central nervous system and the neuroendocrine system as an interpreting transmitter between experience and disease. Whether we are talking of the central nervous system or the immune system we find that where there is an inadequate defense against a destructive experience the result is a heightened vulnerability. Studies have shown that when stressful events place an extraordinary demand on the physiological and psychological defenses, there is a link with an increased vulnerability to the onset of allergic, auto-immune, infectious and neoplastic diseases. This may lead us to the commonly held view that some people, being more vulnerable than others to certain diseases, may be "disease prone," "infection prone" or "cancer prone." It may mean that some are more prone than others to the suppression of their immunological resistance.

This proneness may have its origins in the uterus. A mother's health, emotional state and behavior affect the child long before it is born. From earliest days after birth, the child's resistance and coping style will be influenced by the parents' way of managing their stresses. Vulnerability is inevitably affected by the family into which a child is born — hereditary factors, the family's history of dealing with stress, the patterns of bonding and the information flow within the family networks and systems. We know that prior experiences with distressing events and noxious stimuli help to establish a level of tolerance both physically (as a person resists infection or invasion) and emotionally (as a person feels better equipped to weather the recurring storm). Certain coping styles and personality characteristics become important components in this tolerance. Attitudes also play a part — attitudes which sustain a person's sense of control over life's events and provide a sense of meaning to what is happening, and which are effective in interpreting stresses as challenges rather than as oppressive problems.

A person becomes vulnerable to diffuse emotional and body reactions when they cannot resolve their conflicts, are being torn in several directions and experience heightened and sustained fear and anxiety. Their conflicts may not always be accessible to them — they may not recognize them — for often it is only after considerable exploration that they discover the underlying conflicts which have provoked their body symptoms and sickness.

A 45-year-old ex-priest was dying of lung cancer. He had never smoked, but in the year before his death he developed an irritable cough, which was generally unrelieved by any form of treatment. Several tests were carried out but there was no indication of any physical malignancy. Five weeks before he died, he underwent a bronchoscopic examination which revealed substantial established tumors in both lungs. He had been in intermittent psychotherapy during the year prior to this examination. As his death approached, I asked him if he made any connections between his fatal condition and other aspects of his life.

Without hesitation, he said, "I would never have thought it possible, but I see how my curtailment of my anger has brought my early death." He was angry at the way the Church had treated him and he was angry at his upbringing where overtly expressed anger was subject to strong reactions. He had also been through three intimate relationships, where his frustration and anger were frequently aroused and could find no adequate acceptable expression.

A process of destructiveness may take over a person,

and they become vulnerable to their own persistent self-devaluation, self-blame, punitive wishes and apparent obsessive persecution. They may become overly scrupulous about doing what is right and about all the wrongs they have done in the past. It is as if they have an inner taskmaster that needs to be tamed, and taught how to be more loving and supportive of its valued host! Instead, parts of the person seem to declare war on the well-being and health of the whole person. Anger and rage become examples of alexithymia, which is an inability to find words for feelings. Instead of being directed to an appropriate outer object, the anger and rage become directed to the person. This may be because they believe they are guilty and bad and deserve to be punished. It may be because they see in themselves something of the outer bad object, or it may be they are confused about their anger and have no idea how to control or manage it effectively. The person may become involved in destructive behavior such as overeating, alcohol and drug abuse, they may develop serious physical symptoms or they may neglect their basic hygiene. Interested audiences may demand that they act differently but they, in their apparent diffuse or learned helplessness, proceed with their self-attack and self-destructiveness.

Inevitably, the way people perceive the stresses of their life, interpret them and give them meaning, affects how they will feel and behave in relation to those stresses. Their ways of thinking, their imagination and memory, distortions and irrationalities, can provoke states of unease, apprehension and fear which play out their effects in behavior and body reactions. The way they think and react in regard to life, and their part in it, begins to become a way of life. As they bring together particular ways of thinking and reacting, they start to see patterns

and personalities taking shape, and may show vulnerabilities to specific illnesses. The person who worries may
develop gastric ulcers; those caught up with intense rage
and anger may be at risk of heart attacks, and so on.

Various traumas can affect the immune system and
provoke a vulnerability to illness and disease. A critical
factor in this may be the meaning we give to those
traumas, the way we see ourselves and our own resources
and what we imagine or fear may happen. At times the
image of an anticipated or feared event may evoke a diffuse reaction greater than if the event actually occurred.

A man, aged 43, attended three funerals in six months,
all of them for colleagues approximately his own age. He
was shocked by the loss of his three close friends in such
a short time. He dwelt on how unusual it was for one
person to attend three funerals in so short a time. (He
overlooked that a funeral director may attend as many
funerals in one day, but because of a different attitude and
involvement had no difficulty in coping.) He began to
ruminate on the death of his friends and on his own
death. Some minor stomach pains were quickly magnified
in his thinking. He began to turn the pages of popular
medical magazines. He developed early morning diarrhea
and during the day he was in a constant state of fear of
losing control of his bowels while in an important meeting. He would perspire freely, and found difficulty in
thinking clearly and making considered judgments.

Other traumas that may affect our body reactions vary
from the prospect of approaching retirement or a sense of
demoralization, to the sudden loss of a spouse, involvement in a disaster or major surgery that restricts functioning capacities. Some people withstand multiple traumas,
but then one particular trauma (an insult, a son leaves
home, an injustice) becomes "the straw that breaks the

camel's back." The defenses break down and the person succumbs to a distressing physical illness.

One man had been through the concentration camps of Europe. Later, he had a displaced-person status in four countries. Eventually he went to Australia where he endured humiliating discrimination. He learned the English language, married and helped rear a family of four children. It was only when his second daughter told him that she was going to get a divorce, to marry a man with whom she had had a private relationship for three years, that this man began to collapse. He became depressed and had two coronary occlusions before he realized he was converting his long-standing and current sadness and rage into symptoms that could destroy him.

One man in his late forties had had a strained and disillusioning relationship with his wife. When he became tense he also realized how helpless he was to achieve the goals he had always entertained in his marriage. His professional community expected that he would demonstrate the values of a good marriage. For years he would overeat as a way of finding acceptable satisfaction and of expressing his frustration. His excess weight became his outward expression of his overt happiness in the world, and his inward expression of his helplessness and self-denigration.

He readily connected his behavior with experiences in his early childhood. "My mother was deprived of warmth and affection and so obviously used food to draw the three children closer to her. Here I am forty years later, still using food as a solace or symbol of intimacy, and also something that destroys my self-respect."

After a long period of ambivalence his wife left the marriage. Three months later, he had a cardiac arrest and died.

During his lifetime this man found that the tensions and stress of his marital relationship drove him to eat and he developed body reactions and conditions that ultimately killed him. He perceived that his own values and those of his environment did not allow him sufficient ways to resolve his frustrations. He resorted to the aggressive behavior of childhood, induced by an intimacy-deprived mother. His early learning and early environment were influential factors in the way he converted his later frustrations and relationship trauma into body symptoms. As Edgar Levenson (1978) wrote, "in the simplest sense one becomes what one has experienced" (p. 572).

Vulnerability may develop out of a sense of growing despair and the apprehension that no change is possible or there is no way out. It is common to find that people "give up on life," develop destructive despairing behavior, capitulate and die. Many accept what is happening to them as inevitable. When it could have been possible to establish a resistance, adopt a new life-style, develop a program appropriate to the new reality, they instead docilely accept the situation, embrace negative stereotypes, succumb to an ineffective life-style or sick role and look forward to death. This kind of vulnerability may arise not only from the person, but from the human environment in which they live — their interpersonal relationships, the qualities and expression of support and care, the sense of having no room to move, no purpose in living and no stimulation for imagination and vitality.

Unfortunately some of our environments make people highly vulnerable to despair, depression, illness and disease. In some instances people have sought treatment for their condition and the treatment itself has made them vulnerable to a new range of hazards. Their medication for one condition made them feel so dreadful that they thought they were going mad, and without being aware of it, they placed their lives at risk. These are sometimes called iatrogenic conditions: they arise out of the diagnosis or treatment or the manner of the doctor. We tend to overlook or avoid seeing the part that physicians, therapists and professional helpers play in provoking vulnerability and further conditions of anxiety, destructiveness and sickness.

The Significance of Body Symptoms and Reactions

It can be instructive to explore the significance that certain body reactions and body organs have. When a person is suffering, an urgent goal is to relieve the suffering. That can be done without a thought being given to the meaning or the underlying significance of the suffering. At other times we may find that there is a great deal more to be heard as we listen to what the symptoms and sickness may be saying.

Many people have died because they did not receive treatment for the underlying loneliness and inner pain of which their physical sickness was a symptom. Others became incapacitated because an underlying fear and distortion fueled an imagination that made coping with the ordinary tasks of life impossible.

Body symptoms become a communication — to interested audiences, to the world, to the fantasy we have of others, to God, to the self.

"I am sick."

"I am in trouble."

"I can't help myself."

"The world is unjust."

"See what you are doing to me."

"If you loved me I would not be like this."

"I dare not admit I can't cope, but I can claim some assistance if I'm sick."

"It's all a mess."

"I can never get over this."

"I'm doomed to a low-level existence."

"I made an error and there's no way of getting it right."

"If people see me sick they'll look at me and treat me in a different way."

Body symptoms may hide an inner searching and sadness. There is a sense of lost effectiveness and lost potential.

A woman, aged 52, married with two adult children, complained of cramps in the chest, frustration and general misery. She knew she had a potential that could not be realized. She searched for an intimacy that she knew she could never find. She looked at the quality of mothering she had provided for her two daughters. She said she had never been sufficiently free and spontaneous to provide the warmth and consistency that should have characterized her love for her children. "I think I blame my own parents for what happened to me." She was in search of parents who would provide her with stable, secure affection. Instead her body symptoms were anguished cries for attention, and although her husband provided ample attention, she continued to feel frustrated and empty.

Some say that body reactions are a search for the mother, and the warmth and tenderness associated with the mother; others say they are the search for the father, the masculine, the strength and tenderness that can be associated with the father. The search is probably at a deeper level: a longing for confirmation of one human being by another, a yearning for an assurance that the world is ultimately a loving world, a striving for something outside the self, and embraced within the self, of a good contact and a comfortable connection.

Body reactions represent a concealed wish, which can work in several ways. They can be expressions of a wish to succumb, to be dependent or to die. It is sometimes expressed openly in such words as "Why should I go on trying?" or "I might as well throw in the towel ..." or "We all die sooner or later." It may also be expressed more subtly: "It's lonely being on your own" or "I don't have much to live for."

Body reactions may also be a wish for punishment, a wish to give full expression to those things which for so long have been held in abeyance. There may be a wish to be looked after, rewarded and honored in ways that did not occur in earlier years. Unfortunately this wish is sometimes counterproductive in that the people whose attention is sought do not respond in desirable ways and in any case, the symptoms may be too destructive. At another level, the wish may be to find some union for one's sense of disillusionment and alienation, a wish to return to an intimacy and a dependency that was once lost, or to a union with God, where, as the Book of Revelation described:

He will wipe away every tear from their eyes, and death shall be no more, neither shall there be mourning nor crying nor pain any more, for the former things have passed away (Revelation 21:4).

Body symptoms may signify that the once stable state is breaking down. Physical resistance, the immune system of the body, emotional resources and psychological hardiness and resilience are all involved, and when strained too far, the body may begin to show the signs of wear and tear and break down. The person experiences various alarm reactions, which are followed by deliberate efforts to move out of the stressful zone. But if this proves too difficult, or the stresses remain at a high level, then exhaustion is likely to follow.

A person who develops body symptoms and destructive behavior may do so out of a concealed sense of helplessness and rage. This may have connections with the parents' management of helplessness or rage, and the way they used or accepted illness and body reactions as part of their interpersonal transactions. It could work both ways — illness could be used as an expression of rage and as a way to control others, or it could be a cry for help, for closeness, warmth, consolation and deliberate care.

One elderly man said his strongest memory of his mother was her continual rushing as if she at no time wanted to be close to anyone, but he and his brother discovered — as children — that the one time she would stop and ask what was the matter with them was when they showed they were ill. It became a mode of behavior throughout their life: when they felt they had lost contact, or were up against such odds that threatened to erode their outward show of strength, they would become ill. Their body reactions provided an approved way of being weak and vulnerable, and seeking attention and some solace.

Body symptoms may appear in body organs which have acquired symbolic or unconscious significance. A person may develop an illness that is a symbol of the deprivation he suffered from his mother. Some women may too readily agree to a hysterectomy; it becomes a symbol of their identification with others who have had a hysterectomy and it can be a symbol of their own self-perception. Some organs of the body may unconsciously be given significance — a person may develop a pain in the neck because unconsciously they regard themselves, or other people, as a pain in the neck. Dizziness, coughing, the sense of choking or severe headaches may mean that certain zones of the body have become targets for unconscious conflict and anxiety.

One woman, throughout her married life of thirty years, rejected her husband and the intimacy he both offered and wanted. She was anxious and frightened about getting too close to people. She felt people would always "let you down." To help defend herself against the anxiety of loneliness and intimacy, she strenuously advocated the posture and practice of independence and self-sufficiency. She eventually developed a serious illness that permanently incapacitated her. She had to rely on her family completely for her feeding, her bed comfort and her body cleaning. At the end of her life she succumbed to an existence where intimate caring was required several times a day and during the night. Unconsciously she was testing what she had always feared.

The body symptoms may help to reduce an unbearable tension and they may provide a valued detachment from inner psychic pain. We have seen that a great deal of time and energy may be vested in the body symptoms without any attention being given to the inner tension and pain. A person may not be aware of what is happening within their own organism, or within their interpersonal relationships, but their symptoms may reveal how extensively they may have been damaged and how urgently they need care to prevent further destruction.

A man and his wife had raised five children within a relationship that was repetitively loaded with frustration. The husband was very sensitively affected by the tension that existed, and by the disillusionment he felt that his ideals within a close relationship could not be fulfilled. His wife was openly hostile and vindictive. They both became heavy drinkers and were regularly drunk. It was their way of becoming involved in an array of apparently inconsequential but destructive pursuits, which gave them and the audiences the impression that "everything was under control."

Body symptoms may be an unconscious form of self-punishment and self-negation. A person with a low self-image may use their symptoms as a way of punishment and to reinforce low self-image. They may not be aware of the nature of the extent of this punitive inner action that strikes at the sense of failure and inferiority. They may remember and recall earlier events and punishments, and adopt a way of being that reflects their subjugate status.

Body reactions may be a form of identification with another person. While a son is away at the war a mother in her anxiety may suffer anxiety and pain as a result of loss, but she may also imaginatively identify herself with what she believes would be her son's suffering. Others suffer vicariously — they take on the suffering of others. This may be a conscious wish, but it may often be unconscious and irrational. Long after a person has died, some people continue to suffer, as if suffering for them and instead of them.

Body symptoms can become so deeply part of daily behavior that they are accepted as a way of life. Some people are disgusted at themselves; others use their symptoms to gain certain goals and to avoid discomfort and pain. But many settle for the fact that their various ailments or behavior disorders reflect who they are, and become their way of life. This can be justified by saying "I'm not suffering as much as my father did" or "I know it is not nearly as distressing as the suffering of some people." Thus they compare themselves with others; they look at their own biography; they call on their memory of past suffering and the suffering of others. They formulate a picture of themselves, their resources and their future.

Body symptoms may reflect anxiety and pain of past relationships, present relationships, the environment, society generally or a particular sector or traumatized zone of the world. The anxiety and distress may be displaced onto and confused with the body. Symptoms may also reflect the nature and tone of the environment or the transitions of life.

A person may feel understimulated and underutilized; they may perceive themselves as discarded and of no further worth. On the other hand they may perceive themselves as overstressed by their environments, over-committed and overstimulated. Body symptoms may provide time-out, a retreat, a different pace and an opportunity to assess and negotiate what is happening as far as their relationship and environment stresses are concerned.

Body symptoms are usually outside a person's voluntary control. The person may be deeply affected by their fear — fear that something must have happened in the past, fear that something is going to happen, fear of what is the matter with them and fear of what is the matter with their environment or the world. Their coping capacity is affected. They can no longer function effectively and

142 · Life After Loss

they may feel they cannot go on. Their symptoms become a way of standing still, a breakdown of expectation and the sense of who they are or what they are meant to be. A great deal of pressure is put on them to change but this can accentuate their already established experience of helplessness and ineffectiveness. It also overlooks how serious these symptoms can be. If people could get rid of them, and if they could find some effective way to live more comfortably, they would generally choose to do so.

What to Do About Body Reactions

People frequently ask what they can do about their body reactions and the way their emotional distress and pain and their conscious and unconscious conflicts are expressed. Here are my suggestions:

1   Our first objective is to establish what these body symptoms are. We might accept the assumption that body symptoms are connected with emotional pains and then not proceed to a more accurate definition and diagnosis of the symptoms and the underlying distress and pain. The fact that the body reactions have connections with emotional pain does not mean that they are not in need of treatment. Some symptoms are such threats to life and well-being that urgent intervention is vital.

2   Some body symptoms and sicknesses are less troublesome and less invasive once their connections and causes have been identified. These connections may be buried far into the past, or may be concealed and confused by both past and current events. By recognizing the connections a person assumes a better self-

understanding, and a stronger sense of control over the events and experiences of their life.

3   Body reactions may be reduced in their intensity and pervasiveness as ways are found to recognize the emotional energy, and as other means to manage it are found. People may look carefully at the stressors of their life and how they are coping with them. By changing their coping methods (for example, by using a different way of thinking, by effectively using distractions, by practicing meditation and relaxation) they will find they are less likely to express themselves through sickness and body reactions.

4   Habit patterns, environments of acceptance and particular relationships become established over periods of time. Body reactions and the sickness mode of life may become part of these. To reduce or modify these reactions it will be necessary to change the habits, environments and relationships. Sometimes the symptoms may be serving such an important unconscious purpose that people would die rather than relinquish the symptoms and face life without them.

5   Body reactions inevitably affect a person's self-esteem and self-confidence. A higher image of self provides the person with a sense of stronger resources to combat the tendency to become sick, and to establish a more effective stance for recovery. A stronger sense of self also enhances the person's immunity.

6   It may be necessary or helpful to gain release from self-imposed sanctions, distressing memories and unfinished business. While it is not possible to complete business with people who are no longer accessible, the tendency to do that work inside

the body has to be strenuously and persistently rejected. The inner problems are brought fully into awareness, reduced to a size and form which are manageable and, where possible, converted into realistic achievable tasks.

7 A judgment has to be made whether the person will be the focus of concern for corrections to be made, or whether their interpersonal environment will be the major focus of concern. It may be appropriate to identify the nature of the losses within the environment, and reshape and reorganize the meanings and the emotions that have gathered around them. The perpetuation of negative thoughts and self-destructive anger requires vigorous intervention. The anger reaction can be examined for its validity, its appropriate expression, the alternatives and the consequences — always ensuring that the person is not a victim of capricious emotions, but has a capacity to exercise some control over their expressions and their impact.

8 A great deal of care is necessary as people explore and express their feelings. Some therapists may believe the discharge of emotion will be beneficial. This is not always so. An inappropriate arousal of some feelings may precipitate a diffuse and anxious reaction. Their vulnerability may be greatly increased, and their condition become worse.

One patient, dying of cancer, said that after her doctor spoke with her about her anxiety over her children, she felt that she would soon die. Her morale collapsed, her pain became persistently more intense and she began to hemorrhage again.

Another person did not know what to do about the anger his therapist had uncovered. He felt guilty, disgusted and ashamed but he also felt agitated and homicidal. He said he went home from his therapy session and felt terrible for three days. "Anything could have happened," he said.

9 The presence of helpful support groups or therapy groups can be a valuable resource as people permit themselves a greater self-awareness and self-exploration. A group allows them to look at what they are doing to themselves and others, and to explore alternatives within a trusted and valued supportive atmosphere.

10 There is a need to examine cultural and social norms that give high credence to physical symptoms. Our norms attach far greater value and prestige to the treatment of bodily ailments than to the prevention of those ailments. Our culture places constraints on the ways emotions are able to be expressed, on the nature of interpersonal relationships and on what can occur within them. In endorsing certain kinds of relationships between men and women, our culture gives little attention to the pain and costs that those relationships incur. We are prepared to spend heavily on ailments and death and little on the construction of different human environments where wider interpersonal satisfactions and emotional expression are facilitated and enjoyed. We need to explore new life-styles which embrace creativity, leisure pursuits, distractions and enhancements that evoke a will to live with a strong coherent expectancy about the future.

9

How Will We Behave?

Then a little old woman grew bold, unknotted her white hair, gave a piercing cry and took farewell of Manolios:

"The name of this fine young man was written on the snow; The sun has risen, the snow has melted and has borne away the name upon the waters."

A few moments later, Pope Fotis raised his hand, and gave the signal for departure: "In the name of Christ," he cried, "the march begins again; courage, my children!"

And again they resumed their interminable march towards the East.

Nikos Kazantzakis

Loss and grief and preoccupation with distressing memories can have both temporary and long-term effects on our behavior. Kind friends and sympathetic support groups may be understanding, and accommodate wide levels of incongruent and maladaptive behavior. But they may also strengthen the grieving person's behavioral confusion and inefficacy or they do little to help the person actively revoke their grieving behavior.

Our aim is to help the person return to health-enhancing and life-affirming behavior as quickly as possible. I reiterate that the long-term process frequently regarded as necessary for grieving has to be challenged, especially when that time lag leaves the person to stagger through their grief in the best way time will allow. We want to develop ways whereby people can reclaim adaptive behavior, and be strengthened in their wisdom and resilience as a result of the traumatic experience they have endured. This goal will not be achieved easily; there is a reluctance to leave well-accepted behavior and there is a strong resistance to embrace quickly a behavior that may be interpreted as in some way betraying or abandoning the person who has died, or as diminishing to the self. The new behavior aims to enhance the self, but there are strong influences that would deny this.

Laura was 61 years old when her husband, Colin, died. Everyone said how well she "coped" with the death and the funeral. They had lived on their own since their last child had married eleven years earlier. Laura filled her day by doing the shopping, cleaning and cooking for Colin. In fact, she fussed and fiddled with a wide range of trivia, but always with one eye open for Colin's whims. After he died, all of these actions and activities lost their point. She often felt very tired and would go to her bed for two or three hours each afternoon. When people would call, she would regularly complain about her tiredness, which soon also included various aches. With the encourage-ment of her callers, she began to believe she may not be well. She began weekly visits to her doctor. One behavior generalized to another behavior, one confirmed the other, one reinforced the other.

After an assessment of these cycles of behavior, she was advised to intercept the patterns which had become accepted as necessary. She had to break with those grief behaviors of going to bed, reinforcing her tiredness and having discussions with people who kept reminding her of her low troughs. Instead, it was important for her to adopt behavior of a functioning person, of how she would imagine she would like to be.

We frequently accept a wide range of so-called grief behaviors as the norm. We nod and say, "Yes that sort of behavior is expected." In recent times there were those who would go on and identify the stage of grief the person had reached, designated by the behavior they were exhibiting.

If our aim is to change behavior, it is vital to identify the behavior that stands in need of change. The grieving person resists this on the grounds that this behavior, or that, is normal — "isn't it?"

The behavior includes persistent crying, social withdrawal, low job functioning, low relationship participation and enjoyment, irritability, sleeplessness, hostility, concentration difficulty, fewer positive interpersonal gestures to a narrower range of people, uncontrolled self-disclosures. Actions reflect a self-appraisal that is not able to cope, unworthy and negative. There is low input into the wider community, no desire or capacity to seek out stimulating experiences. These people tend to gather around them more stressful life events, focusing on deficits in themselves, in others and in the environment.

Many of these behaviors arise directly from the traumatic event or its distressing memory. These behaviors are commonly dormant in the person or embedded in their society's attitudes and models. How do people know how to behave at times of loss and grief? They usually behave in ways they have seen others behave. There are the models, the awareness of various audiences, the behavior that is perceived to be acceptable.

One man sought to remarry three months after his first wife died. He was told this would be unacceptable behavior. He argued that the time factor was not relevant, but nevertheless he acquiesced. There is a great deal of folklore about rebounds, appropriate time lapses and behavior acceptable from people at life's different milestones. We sometimes too categorically become over-concerned about specific incidents without seeing them in their broader context.

I once saw a surf-lifesaver attempt to rescue a man in his late fifties who had been caught in an undertow and carried out to sea. A life-saver was quickly on his board and competently made his way through the high water until he reached the exhausted drowning man. Within seconds, it seemed, he had him back on the beach and was attempting to put life back into his chest as he administered mouth-to-mouth resuscitation and cardiac massage. The man showed no response and by the time the ambulance arrived he was dead.

On that very small part of a very large beach, a few of us gathered to witness a young man's efforts to reclaim the life of a swimmer who had ventured into water which was beyond his capacity. It seemed to us that the whole world had suddenly focused on that small spot on the beach.

It was our total concern. Yet only three or four yards away the vast Pacific Ocean roared on. The sand on which we stood was part of the ocean beach that stretched as far as the eye could see, and encircled the whole of the coastline.

The event of this man drowning on this particular spot led me to reflect on our grief reactions. For a short time we are like the event on the beach. It is the only thing that matters but not far away are the reminders that this event and our behavior are part of the wider ocean and wider beach. We leave the spot and the event is placed in competent hands; the beach remains and the ocean roars on.

With our grief behavior we observe ourselves. It is as if we have an observing self, noting that our behavior is not up to par, and at the same time, that observing self is part of a wider awareness. We are our own awareness and we have come to recognize that when the "not up to par" behavior settles, or a balance is restored, we can become aware of our part in that wider awareness called life itself. And we look to be strengthened by that awareness. In a sense we are dealing with a localized phenomenon against the background of life as a totality, just as the rescue worker was attending to his section of the swimming area against the background of the vast Pacific Ocean. As soon as the local phenomenon is dealt with, and is no longer a total preoccupation, he reverts to that wider continuing reality of the ocean's flow. When this takes place — as also in grieving behavior — people experience their continuity and identity with that larger context, the Ocean, Life, Courage, God. Thus when we ask "How will we behave?" we are asking about more than a fragment of behavior. We are asking about behavior in context, behavior that is both localized and a bridge to experience transcendence.

During the course of their lives, people develop a learned resourcefulness. They learn control and regulation of thoughts, feelings and behavior. They learn coping skills to meet stressful situations. They develop a self-esteem and self-efficacy. This expectation will influence whether a person will initiate coping behavior, how much time and energy he will expend and how long he will continue in the face of troubled and aversive experiences.

Learned resourcefulness and experienced and expected self-efficacy are in contrast to learned helplessness. Martin Seligman (1975) drew attention to the ways in which people learn to believe, and behave as if, they have no control over life events or their reactions to them. They expect bad things to happen, and they do not expect to be able to prevent them from happening. They see the cause and control of such events as being outside their capacity. Demoralization and depression become their known and learned reactions to this helplessness.

This is common in grief. It is therefore necessary to take steps to intercept learned helplessness and to reinforce learned resourcefulness.

Coping behavior and skills relevant to this learned resourcefulness would include:

1 Learning through experience with frustration, and coping with obstacles
2 Learning task-oriented behavior and problem-solving through instruction, conditioning and modeling
3 Developing the capacity to evaluate, to give positive meaning to events and to hold a long view.

Repeatedly we hear people say: "I am just so pleased I had that experience. I learned such a lot from it — Tom and Charles were great models and a source of great encouragement and stimulation. They helped change the whole event. After we had talked with them, we knew we would get through this. It looked different. And we were starting to cope."

Some people in coping with their distress have an internal model, an ideal, a sense of themselves being competent. Other people may place greater emphasis on external models and on external sources of inspiration. These can be identified in the contemporary environment, in literature, in the Scriptures or in the context of religious faith and the religious community. People develop various forms of internal evaluation and conditioning. Certain models and behavior are designated good and are rewarded through the satisfactions experienced, the reassurances conveyed through attitudes and beliefs, and the strengthening and enhancement of their lives.

At times of loss and grief, self-efficacy and resourcefulness are threatened and the ordinary and accepted coping skills and models may be perceived and experienced as irrelevant or inadequate. Anxiety is aroused and behavior can become uncontrolled and diffuse. Some anxieties and maladaptive behaviors arise from distortions, misinformation and misconceptions. It may be appropriate to make the necessary corrections and to encourage the person to move in a direction and into an environment where such misconceptions will not be of foremost concern. Some beliefs may be impervious to any correction; for example, the person may believe they are unworthy and that nobody sees them as significant. Reassurance may be ineffective. Other beliefs and behavior may be the primary focus of concern, rather than those particular irrational beliefs at that time.

June's Mother

A 54-year-old woman was referred to me by her family doctor. He said she had excellent health until approximately eighteen months earlier when she began to report digestive and gastric problems, severe cramping in the stomach followed by extensive episodes of diarrhea. Inevitably the persisting condition affected her ability to work, her social life, her moods, her sleep patterns. At first her husband was concerned and supportive, but he had become irritable and impatient with her frequent and prolonged visits to the toilet. He also became furious with her that every time any of their friends would telephone, she would go into long descriptions of her bouts of pain and diarrhea. The family doctor had her admitted to the hospital twice for observation and for tests and exploration. Nothing could be found to account for her distressing symptoms. At length the doctor said it was "nerves," and since the problem was extending into other areas of her life she should seek some different form of help.

This woman was suffering from delayed stress reaction. Six months prior to the emergence of her first physical symptoms, her daughter had died. Her daughter had been living in Kingston, Ontario, with her husband and two small children. They were not good letter writers but they would phone from Canada every few weeks for short conversations to assure the parents that all was well. Then Douglas phoned to tell the mother that her daughter had suffered a cerebral aneurysm the day before and had died. There had been no indication of any prior distress. Douglas and the children had been in the park on Sunday afternoon; they had returned home and found June already dead.

The parents in Melbourne, Australia, were thrown into confusion, helplessness, guilt and grief. They thought they should fly to Canada for her funeral but they did not have that kind of money. They thought Douglas should come home but he had no job in Melbourne.

"Home for us must be now in Kingston," he said.

"But the children!" the mother protested.

"Don't worry," Douglas said firmly. "We will manage."

He had never been gentle with his mother-in-law; one strong reason for moving to Canada was for them to put some distance between June and her mother. There had been long-standing tension between them.

For six months after June's death her mother walked around in an angry daze. She was very tense and always in a hurry. She then began to develop the distressing stomach problems for which she sought her doctor's help. By the time she sought help with her several reactions and symptoms to her daughter's death, two years had elapsed.

I asked her if she thought she had got over her daughter's death. She replied, "I don't think I'll ever get over it."

I asked her if her friends ever spoke about June. "No," she said, "they never mention her. I think they know how painful it is for a mother to live with something like that."

"But," I said, "you are not *living* with it; you are *dying* with it."

"Is it as bad as that?" she asked.

I suggested she listen very carefully to what she could be doing to herself, how she was in severe pain and distress, how that was forcing her more and more into a role of withdrawal. I put these suggestions to her in a way that she could readily agree with them. I then began to make the bridge from her current pain to her earlier unresolved states.

"You are very irritable and angry. Your husband annoys you. People get under your skin. To some extent you are off-loading your anger toward Douglas onto them, your anger toward fate and God, onto them ... maybe also your anger against June.

"You have told me you had not enjoyed a relaxed and easy relationship with June. She and Douglas had taken your only grandchildren off to Canada. Now she has died, and I imagine you are already thinking Douglas will marry again and you will not see your grandchildren again ..."

She interrupted: "Oh yes, his mother let slip the other day that Douglas could be thinking of getting married again. He's one who knows how to look after himself."

Our conversation continued. As it did we were able

to list the behaviors which required her attention. The difficult decision for her was whether she wanted to change her behavior. Her physical symptoms had become so distressing that she said, "I know I *have* to do something, so I'll do it."

We listed the behaviors that required changing and extinction:

1 Her constant ruminations on June, and why she died
2 Her anger toward Douglas that was so unamenable to any suggestions
3 Her anger toward both of them for going to Canada — if this terrible event was to happen, it would have been better to have happened nearer "home"
4 Her irritability with her husband
5 Her constant reliving of her daily irritabilities before she tried to sleep at night
6 Her persistent adoption of the role of a mourning mother
7 Her mood states and her acceptance of their inevitable negative impact on her various communities
8 The secondary gain and reinforcement she derived from that negative impact
9 Behavior which made withdrawal from her job requirements seem appropriate
10 Behavior which made her social withdrawal seem appropriate
11 Behavior which made her doctor her weekly friend
12 Her persisting diarrhea, requiring a range of behaviors that simultaneously attempted to placate the condition and reinforce it
13 Her repetitious conversations about her condition, which tended to reinforce her social withdrawal and give it a social validation

14   Her contact with people (like Douglas's mother) who had the potential of exacerbating the condition

15   Her anxiety about her condition — this anxiety tended to provoke a fresh cycle of the condition

16   Her readiness to accept her depressed state with its closed-door attitude toward seeking external stimulation, exercise or the planning and disciplining of her body and mind states, and of her food intake

17   Her behavior that was more preoccupied with continuing her body symptoms and their associated moods than with the urgent need to accept her daughter's death and decide to recommit herself to her own life and to life in its broadest sense.

Reorganizing ways of behavior may follow several pathways that call for the person's repetitive recommitment. In the past there has been such an aversive attitude to loss and death that people in their distressed reaction are largely left to the healing processes of time or they are encouraged to continue to "work on" or "work through" their grief — almost to wallow in it — until it is dissipated. If it did not dissipate they had to accept it as their role in life, confirmed by folklore and the statements of many with good intentions: "You never get over these things." Not everyone turns to their doctor or psychologist in their grief stress reaction. The people to whom they turn usually have no explicit theory to guide them and hence their help will not maximize the possibilities of relieving or extinguishing the distressing behavior as quickly as possible.

June's mother had developed a wide range of maladaptive behaviors; it would not be surprising that eventually she would have become seriously incapacitated or would have died. Long before a person reaches this stage, some change of behavior is possible. Some are able to follow many of these procedures themselves, and some require instruction and supervision.

Common custom once was for the minister to visit a widow perhaps once or twice after the funeral; perhaps more often if she were young and attractive. Generally those visits demonstrated support and acceptance, but rarely did they confront or challenge maladaptive behavior. In the last two decades this form of visiting has been less evident: widows and widowers are at work during the day and not amenable to grief counseling in the evenings. A growing tendency has been to recommend books and pamphlets for reading. These books and pamphlets usually reflect more of society's inability to make any sense of death than its intention that people should be restored to the mainstream of life as soon as possible.

Behavior change sets out before us such a goal. It requires a commitment. It could require several closely spaced practice-consultations, preferably every third day, over a period of three to four weeks. The procedure does not follow a set sequence but could include the following (using June's mother as an example).

June's mother had never adequately faced the reality of her daughter's death. She had become so entangled with anger and guilt that she had not actually severed the bond. Her psychic energy was still invested in June even though June was dead. That investment was not hard to understand since June had been absent though alive for some time. It was difficult to make the transition to see June absent and dead, and to recognize that the energy tied up in that bond or attachment over many years had to be withdrawn, reorganized and changed. June's mother was instructed to schedule half an hour each day for the specific purpose of doing some mourning. This strategy, which amounts to "forced" mourning, brings the person to do something about that energy which otherwise would remain diffuse and out of control.

Her ruminations about June and Douglas, and the future that Douglas would now provide for the grandchildren, had become destructive and ineffective. It also persistently led to hostility and irritability and depressive mood states. It was important for these ruminations and their consequences to be eliminated. She was encouraged to see the ineffectiveness of her ruminations for achieving any positive worthwhile goal. She was instructed to recognize her ruminations and intercept them, to recognize the early signals for the onset of such ruminations and seek a "detour" or a distraction and thus prevent the rumination occurring. I wanted to challenge the strongly held notion that reliving old scenes and ruminating on the past or the dread of the future were necessary for constructive grieving.

She began a systematic self-monitoring in which she recorded in a daily diary the occasions she began to ruminate, the occasions she felt angry and hostile, what provoked these states and how long they lasted. This began to induce an increasing state of self-evaluation and self-control. She was beginning to practice skills gained in the consulting room in other places and this encouraged a sense of self-efficacy, a better mood state and the awareness that these were the positive consequences of her own growing skills.

June's mother had come to accept her own inner reinforcement of her beliefs, her behavior, her mood; she expected and received reinforcement from others. Her husband's negative reinforcement had taken forms which made it positive. She said, "Whenever he reacts like that, it proves I am right." They were usually talking about different issues but the intensity of feelings and threats was such that neither wanted to check what the other was actually talking about.

We set out to change this inner/outer reinforcement pattern. She was instructed in ways of identifying relationships or social conversations and reactions that confirmed her illness or her attitude. She was able to avoid them, intercept them or withdraw from them. She was taught to practice specific sentences that countered overt and incipient reinforcement of her condition. She practiced making statements that were positive indications of her recovery and her affirmation of participating in life again. Instead of long conversations about her condition, she practiced statements that immediately diverted the course of conversation to other topics. When her husband became irritable, she practiced withdrawal instead of hostile rejoinders; she practiced positive suggestions and attributions about herself, the present and the future. All of this required close monitoring, evaluation and endorsement, first from me and then from herself.

We began to develop strategies designed to counter her negative self-concept, her negative expectations and her negative view of life. She came to recognize that depressed and hostile people tended to induce a negative receptivity and mood in the environment. Such people elicited rejection from those with whom they interacted and confirmed their negative self-efficacy. We realized that there would be times when the stresses would overwhelm her, and that she would tend to relapse into a state of helplessness and hostility.

She was encouraged in those times to practice what some have called the "turtle technique" — illustrated in the story of the old turtle instructing a young turtle that when it ran into difficult and stressful situations its shell provided a way to withdraw for a time. Under its shell the young turtle could calm down, reorganize its resources and resolve and consider the best way to respond. It was good to have a place to go where a turtle could relax and contemplate the significance of events in the context of the whole of life.

June's mother was also trained to re-evaluate her stomach cramps, digestive discomfort and diarrhea. She had become so tense and anxious in her expectations about this condition that her work and her sleep also needed to be included in the re-evaluation.

A program of relaxation and gradual desensitization was developed. In the early stages, her first sign of anxiety in the morning was her diarrhea. We drew up a list of her early morning anxieties. She listed that she could not cope with the demands of her husband, that she would not be able to get all her errands done today and meet all the goals of her work schedule, that she had not heard from Douglas, that she should "do something" about the grandchildren, that she might have cancer, that she could feel the stomach cramp coming on, that she would not have any breakfast and so on.

With a relaxation and desensitization program she was able to exercise increasing control over these many anxieties that had become so diffuse in their incapacitating influence.

Several of these anxieties were converted into problems that could be solved. The requirements of her work situation, what she could do about her marriage and what her future relationships would be with her grandchildren had all become part of an invasive anxiety. We began to designate them as specific problems to which problem-solving strategies could be applied.

This required a firm commitment to such an approach, and a persistence in combating her negative beliefs about her capacity to convert her anxiety into problems and then convert the diffuseness of her helplessness into specific and manageable areas and tasks. Problem-solving strategies require a clear designation and formulation of the problem; generating solutions and alternative solutions; imaging those solutions, evaluating and deciding on an appropriate alternative; putting into operation the chosen solution then evaluating and confirming and establishing an inner reward of self-appraisal, attitude and mood.

We were able to use with benefit the strategy called paradoxical intention. She often lived in fear of another stomach cramp and prolonged bouts of diarrhea. At times we were able to practice inducing the state she most feared. By doing this, she gained added control of her functioning.

When she began to fear what Douglas would do in the future, she knew that as she pursued that thought it would rapidly expand into other concerns, and escalate into catastrophic proportions. At various times, when she was in a relaxed state, she would be encouraged to induce her anxiety about the grandchildren and her future relationship with them. She was able to follow the anxiety through to its negative conclusions, to challenge her irrational attitudes and to see what she could do and what she could not do, what was changeable and what was unchangeable, and what range of meanings, attitudes and feelings she could have that would optimize her health and well-being.

June's mother saw that her negative maladaptive behavior could change her various environments. She could choose the environments she wished to enter; she could change environments in which she was already involved; she could create new environments. She saw what an impact joy and sadness could have on the moods and efficacy of herself and others. Persistently we practiced moving away from the sadness zones to the zones of joy.

There is no doubt that the external and internal rewards and reinforcements to stay in negative grief behaviors are persistent and strong. People keep regressing to environments that confirm their role as sufferers or mourners. They readily revert to behavior that provokes those environments to treat them in ways that confirm the role they perceive themselves to be in or to endorse the incompetence and hurt of the self-image they desire or accept as theirs.

Changing to more positive behavior presupposes a capacity and the will to make decisions and commitments. When grief and its associated moods and behaviors can be so pervasive, it was necessary for June's mother to live her life within boundaries, yet knowing that ultimately the boundaries did not hold.

She knew that June had been cremated in Canada, and thus a boundary separated her geographically and in terms of life and death; yet the boundary could vanish. It was as if June was alive in her mother's living room in Melbourne. She knew that the chances of her seeing her grandchildren again were very slender; several boundaries separated them — geographical, experiential, time and orientation. But at times all boundaries would disappear and she would see herself attending her grandchildren's twenty-first birthday parties and their weddings. It was as if she had transcended her own mortality.

A much more acute problem had to be faced in her daily existence. She could not forget her many problems, yet she had to function as a person in a responsible job, as a person accepting that she was going to stay married. At times it was necessary for her to keep the various problems of her life confined within these boundaries that she had to draw. We can use the nautical nomenclature and refer to this as "bulkheading." It means we use a partition to form a watertight compartment and thus prevent flooding from one compartment to another.

June's mother had established the habit of carrying her hassles with her husband into her workplace. At a more fundamental level she was allowing her unfinished business with June and Douglas to flood into all areas of her life until she was drowning, in almost every area of her life. She was able to practice bulkheading to prevent this flooding. She could recognize that the problem with Douglas could only go so far; then she had to leave it, put it in its compartment and move into the zone of life requiring her attention and in which she could be effective.

She would have an angry encounter with her husband. That could be so overwhelming and symbolic of so much of her ineffectiveness that it would seem as if everything was out of her control. But she could make the comparison with the man's death on the beach, mentioned earlier: it was not the end of the world; it was, in fact, only a very small event on a vast beach, a tragedy of limited dimensions when placed in the context of the drama of the ocean and the disclosures of eternity.

No one knew of June's mother's inner conflict. She had reported only her physical symptoms and discomfort. She herself had not realized the nature of the interconnections of her delayed stress reaction. We had to ask her "How will you now behave?" and focused on her maladaptive behavior and on ways of restoring behavior to appropriate levels of satisfaction and security, effectiveness and vitality.

Although we have indicated that this behavior always has an environmental context, an ecological fit, it also has a behavioral economic component. There is a cost-effectiveness in all forms of behavior — the costs are more frequently experienced rather than calculated. Perhaps we fear the actual financial costs and therefore avoid the figures. A person who is host to inner-mind pain and behavioral underfunctioning is a very costly person. As that person moves into various modes of medical or psychological need, the costs rapidly soar.

There are other costs often concealed or muted as far as wider communities are concerned: the costs involved in family depression and morale, marital stress and disintegration. There are costs involved in society's ontological anxiety as it moves to deny or cushion the impact of loss and death, and as it subliminally reinforces noncoping behavior and chronic grief as an acceptable form of adjustment to a particular stress. The ecological balance of the forest is not disturbed when one blind sparrow drops off the branch and falls dead on the ground below. A similar event in human terms can disrupt "a forest" ten thousand kilometers away, as with the effect of June's death on her mother, her mother's husband, work colleagues, friends and health advisers. The costs can be so impacted that not one of the affected people or the various environments knew what stress in June's mother was responsible for such ongoing disruptions.

Costs are not only calculated directly in money. There are costs when relationships are strained, when people are confused, when time and energy are used in destructive ways, when a person is diffusely responding to known and unknown stimuli in several zones at once. Sooner or later pertinent questions have to be asked.

"How long can I go on like this?"

"How long can our human systems tolerate a persistent unresolved disruption?"

"Is it cost-effective in the broadest sense to allow these things to occur?"

"Is it appropriate and health enhancing to the individuals within the various systems? What is it doing to their morale, their view on life, their world-view, their *joie de vivre?*"

And the person might also ask: "Can I afford not to do anything about this?"

Franz and Catarin

Franz and Catarin were not long married when they were swept into the concentration camps of Europe. Their families were wiped out. They were shunted from camp to camp, and survived. On their release they migrated to Australia. After initial problems of adjustment, language and work, and always overshadowed by memories and past horrors, they found their feet.

They had three children. Two were killed in a freak accident on the road when they were six and eight years of age. The other child, a daughter, narrowly escaped, but lived under a shadow of guilt and anxiety. When she was 20, at university, she joined a rebel group and became alienated from her parents and fiercely in opposition to them.

Her parents agonized over this added distress in their lives and tried to do everything possible to keep contact with their daughter, but her anger and distrust continued to flood all of their communications.

Franz and Catarin had a small circle of friends but above all, they drew closer to each other. They had several visits overseas on business and many vacations together. Though so much else had hurt them over their life span, from the age of 50 to 60 they felt they had discovered a rare happiness with each other.

Franz had decided to retire early, at 60. He had sufficient assets to do so. Catarin worried that Franz would be bored or lost without the activities and involvements of his work but he protested that they would have more time to enjoy this phase of life which would be in stark comparison with the dreadful experiences they had been through in their twenties.

Franz was soon at a loose end. He joined a group of other men who were also at a loose end. They fed each other's discontent with the state of the world and Franz was often reminded of earlier days. He began to fear that the world might collapse around him. His ruminations led to depression. His depression led him into excessive distorted perceptions. He fluctuated from low moods to states of tension and agitation. He continued to tell his wife how much she meant to him but she later recalled there were times when he seemed to withdraw from her.

One evening at six o'clock the police called at the door and told Catarin her husband was dead. They had found his body in the locked car on the nearby beach. It was suicide.

Catarin was thrown into a dreadful state. For months she felt she could never cope with this tragedy. She had been so dependent upon him. They had been so close to each other. She could not understand why he would ever do such a thing to himself or to her. She did not know how to exist, how to help herself or what to live for. "Help me come back to life," she said.

She said she was extremely lonely and alone. She felt ashamed. The friends she had, had drifted away. She was able to do some welfare work for the Blind Institute but each day as she walked home she felt a vast emptiness. Tears were uncontrollable.

She and I began the work of reconstruction. Her misery and inner distress were quickly identified as expressions of confusion and anger. She could not make sense out of her husband's actions. We looked carefully at all the evidence she could bring forward: it became increasingly clear that he had gradually slipped into a state of depression. His capacity to make accurate perceptions and judgments deteriorated. Without realizing it he was in the grip of a serious disorder which unless identified and treated would overtake him and prove fatal. Although suicide looks like a willful act based on some appraisal and judgment of a life situation, very often that appraisal and judgment are out of rational control, for the person is already overwhelmed by the fatal depressive illness.

Many people fail to understand the depressed person and the act of suicide. They are perhaps horrified by it or by what they see that it represents. Thus, instead of providing a vital support to the grief-stricken survivors, they begin to move away. The survivors carry a sense of shame until they see that the "shame" arises from their perception of the punitive attitudes of their friends.

Catarin was encouraged to reappraise the friendship of her friends and to see that their fear and evasion could be of no help to her and that their friendship no longer stood. She realized she was then able to re-establish some control of her thinking that had become so out of her control that she had been punishing herself. She saw that she'd had enough posed against her without also attacking herself.

She listed what she was doing to herself. She was continuing to hurt herself; she was going over and over the events trying to derive some meaning from them; she was returning to old photographs which reminded her of how things once were and how she once looked. She saw that her negative thinking overwhelmed her several important positive experiences. So she listed the positives:

1 I am in good health.
2 I am trying to find a new purpose.
3 I am ready to help people; I am basically a caring person.
4 I am much stronger than I had ever thought.
5 I am a very intelligent person.
6 I am a good-looking woman.
7 I have times of positive determination.
8 I am keeping a daily diary to help confirm my progress.

She recognized that her thinking was often negative and outweighed her positive thoughts two to one. She frequently had feelings that were miserable and fed further misery. And her behavior generally followed as noncoping and blocked behavior. She knew she had to focus attention on her thinking, feeling and behavior — so that they would be different.

To do this we had to identify that her thinking, feeling and behavior were expressions of her grief, and her grief provoked and caused her thinking, feeling and behavior.

I then recounted to her how one person I was helping with a similar grief regularly went to her bed each afternoon. There she would ruminate on her misery and pain, her helplessness and despair, and her unsolvable problem.

We decided that her problem was to get over her grief. Her grief was pain. She at once recognized that she had also been going to her bed and that she had been studying old photographs and cards. This behavior was identified as behavior that required change.

She volunteered that she kept a daily diary, but that each day it was full of how the day was a day of sadness, aching and no purpose.

We then set out three stages of her journey. She immediately said that she had to make a leap out of stage one to stage two. Stage one was her negative and grieving behavior, feeling and thinking. The first leap was to cross the gulf to stage two where she began to adopt different thinking, feeling and behavior. She was encouraged to use her diary. At the end of each day, after she had made her regular entry, she would then enter where she had noted a change to a more positive thinking, feeling and behavior. We recognize that the leap is not successful if we only substitute positive thoughts for negative thinking, feeling and behavior. The negative has to be identified and dealt with in ways that reduce its overwhelming influence and its persistent invasive distortions.

Catarin said, "But what about some purpose in life? I have nothing." I urged her to examine her statement in two ways. First, to put it alongside the several actions she performed each day which were purposeful. For example, she took care over her diet; she kept up her appearance; she went out to help people at the Blind Institute; she knew that God knew her life was right and that the tragedies which had befallen her were not due to her malevolence or maleficence. Secondly, she was instructed to reduce her plea for purpose from a large and strong goal and purpose that carried her every day into the future, to a more limited designation of purpose. Purpose was found in small increments of each day.

Catarin was encouraged to look for a moment beyond

stage two, to stage three, where she would be able to tell others in their grief not to go to bed. That is, where she could see that she would no longer be in her present "mess" (as she called it), but would become something of a model for others. She did not reject that possibility.

Aids and Symbols

Beyond the behavioral economics, ecological fit and environmental context, I encourage the person to search out the aids and symbols that will contribute to that changed world-view and changed way of behaving that reflect a stronger sense of identity, autonomy and resilience and an enhanced view of an interdependent humanity striving to find its highest meaning in the context of the "ocean," of Life, of the One, of the Eternal.

Literature is laden with such symbols. There is one unforgettable passage in which David Cairns (1950) tells the story of a young student of his acquaintance who heroically sacrificed his life in saving a boy from drowning. Cairns wrote:

> I want you to realize that scene. You have the whole nature cosmos around you there in symbol, sky and sea and hill and shore, and in the middle of it you have got this deliberate laying of life down. As you look at it you see that this is no unconnected picture. Somehow it is all one whole ... I believe that somehow Nature was there in order that the man might do this thing; that in actions of this kind, and the personalities that lie behind them, lies the clue to the riddle of the world, and the manifestation at once of the source from which that world came, and the end towards which it is working (p. 20).

And so from that sense of purpose he leads on to "the

great fundamental act of Faith in God." There are so many passages of similar beauty and power in this and other books that an anthology might well be made.

And from Nikos Kazantzakis (1963):

> The Captain struggled to his feet in front of the firing squad — He saw him and his young bride visiting his mother in the rocky hills.

> She had waited for them, she waited and waited, since day-break, and now she cried with joy. The newlyweds began to cry too, because they were young and it was spring and the ground smelled sweet; and a partridge that was in a cage in the courtyard paced back and forth behind the bars. It watched the new arrivals and cackled sadly, as though she, too, wanted to be married but her groom was in the hills, and the cage stood between them, preventing their union. She beat against her prison with her beak and her red feet, trying to escape. "Mother," the bride said, "I want to ask a favor of you. I can't stand to see the partridge imprisoned; give me your permission to open her cage and set her free." "She's yours, daughter," the old woman replied, "she's yours to do with as you please." And the bride opened the cage and took the plumed partridge in her palm. She admired her coral legs, the wild, yet gentle, eyes, the puffed-out breast, and quickly she tossed her hand high and released her in the air. "Go on," she told it, "you're free!" (p. 244).

Nature is always ready to play a part as it traverses the seasons, just as the tree, bereft of fruit for years, provides a large harvest this year. The sun rises to bring the light of a new day. The kookaburra laughs for its season in the Australian bush, then it dies and another kookaburra carries the laughter on from bushland to bushland across a country which so often cries in loneliness and pain.

Travel brings its powerful world of different people — of suffering and courage, of squalor and majestic beauty, of desperate helplessness with a language that cannot be understood, and a friendly stranger who steps forward to translate and thereby transform the situation.

Psychotherapy in its several strands has a common theme — that another person listening in a certain way can bring an awareness of a new perspective to the problem and of strengths and skills to deal with the problem; that the meaning a person gives to a situation can be the key to how that situation will be endured; that people can change and cope with situations which were regarded as unchangeable.

The symbols of religion have always been regarded as important for mankind's way of meeting loss and death. Often the power of the symbols has been lost: lost by the need to intellectualize and explain when words can confuse the issues and miss the point. Judeo–Christian religions emphasize the presence of a providential and purposeful God; a good spirit brooding over the turbulent waters, bringing order out of chaos, light out of darkness, hope in times of despair. The symbols of church and cathedral communicate with humanity's desire to lift up eyes and hearts to "the heavenly places," to organize, create and build, and to find in the craftsmanship inspiration and wonder.

Judaism has continued to set forth the symbol of the Passover; Christianity the symbol of baptism, crucifixion and resurrection. Judaism pointed to Moses, and to Abraham, Isaac and Jacob. Christianity pointed to Jesus, Paul, Peter and John and the many apostles, martyrs and saints down the ages who have courageously lived and died in this faith.

Religion sets before people the symbols of the altar, the cross, the color and movement of the people at worship, the art, the drama, the music and the song. Many find religious practices and involvements irrelevant and tire-some — perhaps because the symbols have been con-cealed behind the words and the forms, perhaps because the words and forms and the symbols themselves have lost their meaning or can no longer be adequately explained and interpreted. But in times of loss and death, people might be encouraged to stand quietly before these ancient symbols of cross, altar, scrolls and scriptures, synagogue or church: and let these symbols themselves communicate to their whole being — as life would communicate to life — that attitudes and behavior and life itself might be opened to change.

10
Life-style and the Future

Beware of the past;
Within it lie
Dark haunted pools
That lure the eye
To drown in grief and madness.

James McAuley's translation of
Albrecht Haushofer's sonnet *Warning*

Remember then: There is only one time that is important — Now!
It is the most important time because it is the only time we have any
power.

Leo Tolstoy

Loss of a valued person, like the loss of home or job or status, involves substantial changes in life-style. Sometimes these changes are negative. They become part of a bigger problem, prolong the distress and contribute to a wider destructiveness. At other times these changes in life-style provide opportunities for something new and constructive to occur, with people experiencing a freedom, consciousness and compassion that they had not known before. In managing our losses and griefs we need to give attention to our life-style not only as it is worked out by each of us in our individual ways, but also as it is influenced and facilitated by our particular social context and society in general. Loss can affect the physical and financial structures in far-reaching ways — where we live, whether we continue in the same line of work, the internal domestic arrangements, change in status and mobility.

One family had enjoyed an elaborate life-style. The husband and breadwinner disappeared, taking his vast wealth with him. The house in which his wife and four children lived had to be sold to meet the several large debts that were outstanding. The family which had enjoyed the use of three cars was suddenly reduced to one vehicle. They moved from house to house and eventually moved their belongings to the home of an aged aunt. The mother who had onced moved in the high circles of society had to take regular work to make ends meet. For all of them there had been a substantial change in life-style which was difficult to adapt to and which tended to exacerbate their sense of loss, their helplessness and depression.

In another instance a widow had to take up work on the farm she and her husband had previously managed and owned. The farmhouse was in a very isolated spot on the northeastern interstate border. Her extended and demanding role meant that her isolation was com-pounded by an enforced social withdrawal and the envi-ronment for her three children was — according to her own appraisal — far from stimulating. This changed life-style prolonged her distress and added to her grief. Thus we see how a changed life-style emerges not only from the physical and financial structures but also from the social context and the way we perceive ourselves functioning within that context.

We can become and remain trapped in a life-style and way of behavior without realizing that assumptions behind that behavior no longer hold. Some people con-tinue to act to please their mother long after she is dead, or believe they should continue to behave in certain ways because that is the way the dead person would have liked. James McAuley expressed this in these words:

I am the web in the corner
In which the insects are caught
But the spider lies crushed on the floor.

A woman who lived in a country town became a compulsive eater after her husband died. She became overweight, apathetic, untidy and unexercised. Her moods were marked by irritability and irrationality. Her general life-style alienated her from her family and social relationships. Their recurring avoidance and rejection confirmed her self-evaluations of unworthiness and provoked further eating and self-destructive attitudes.

Her overeating, its consequences and associated moods, were expressions of anger toward a husband who was dead. They were active residues of a past she refused to put to rest. She provoked family reactions and these in turn seemed to justify her behavior and life-style. It became a life-style of increasing self-pity, self-indulgence, self-destructiveness and demoralization. When therapy was ultimately focused on the dynamics of her destructiveness and demoralization, she began to explore alternatives in the context of some persistent reconstruction of the self and the development of a life-style in which she was confronted by choices that had to be made.

Children who have lost a parent through death or divorce not only will have specific reactions to that loss, but will find, as they begin to interpret its significance, the change of life-style involved. This will evoke further reactions of frustration and anger, uncertainty and anxiety, deprivation and loneliness. Children may find they have to assume a parenting role, change their home, live with other families and reorder their way of mixing with their friends. Their participation in the various tasks and events of life will change. Adolescents have more developed inner capacities to understand and appreciate illness and death, and while their reactions may be different from small children's reactions they may be substantially different from the adult reaction. The adult has lost a partner, a wife or husband, a lover, a domestic helper, a social support; the child has lost a parent, a model, a protector, a source of comfort and wisdom. A child's relationship with the parent is unique.

Adults distribute their energies among family, friends, work and leisure pursuits. Young children tend to invest all their energies in their parents. Adolescent children may be at that stage of growth and conflict where energies are divided among the parent and peers. The death of the parent can profoundly affect the adolescent's total experience and life-style. This might involve the style of family life and movement into a different socializing process.

Western philosophy and life-styles have always had difficulty coping with loss and death. The distinctive drawing of boundaries between life and death, the external world and the internal experience, observable behavior and the environment in which the behavior occurs, may have helped our scientific certainties but it has created considerable and philosophical and subjective uncertainty. Psychotherapy has spoken of the way we attach ourselves to our loved objects, of the processes of taking external parent figures into ourselves and of the merging of reality and unreality with some argument about which was which. Religion has spoken about being one with God, of God being a spirit, of the transmogrification of the human spirit, of human life being part of the life of God — the source and ground of all being, of life after death and of a consummation of all things.

It is not surprising then that our life-styles become confused in their values and direction, the understanding of their context and the actualization of their potential. We inflict restraints, beliefs and behavior on each other and on ourselves in the name of growth and social acceptance without recognizing that we are often committed to destruction and pathology. We affirm our quest for happiness and pleasure and simultaneously unconsciously or in ignorance adopt attitudes and behavior that, in the longer view, are injurious to personal health, social dialogue and the ecological balance of things.

When we experience the loss of a significant relationship our own balance is disrupted. We may act as if the problem can be dealt with in the same way as we might change a tire on the car so that as quickly as possible we can continue on our journey without any permanent change being caused by the flat tire. In other words, we try to deal with the loss as something "over there," as an entity or an experience in itself, without any impact on our life-styles or mode of being. We say, "Life has to go on," as if our perception and experience of the balance of things are unaffected by the loss.

While the wider ocean may be imperceptibly affected by the drowning on the Pacific beach, those who are most intimately involved in the network of the drowned man's life and death are affected. It may be that his death will be part of the ongoing daze or it may provoke a reappraisal of life-styles in individuals and the broader social context.

For generations the individual has been seen as an entity apart from their interpersonal social context, their inner attitudes and aspirations. Treatment procedures have frequently been absurdly rigid in excluding the context and interconnectedness, influential people and interested audiences.

There has been a slow acceptance of a dynamic contextual approach to human existence and to the crises and pains that human beings experience. With the fascination of treating specific diseases and with the adoption of the reductionist model that looked for the specific cause and the specific intervention, it has been difficult to make the full transformational shift to a more inductive approach that looks for the meaning and significance of the crisis in terms of a person's comprehensive biology and biography, interpersonal and cultural context, and ecological spirituality. This also involves a shift from seeing the person as a passive responder to causal influences, to seeing the person as an active agent who is able to utilize their own powers of self-control, volition, imagination and behavior to achieve desirable goals. In this regard it is important to explore not only what is happening in the current self but also the "possible selves" (Markus and Nurius, 1986) and how these affect the way people think about what they want to be, their potential and their future. Possible selves may well provide a vital link between the self-concept and motivation insofar as they function as incentives for future behavior and help provide some form of evaluation for the current self and its way of functioning.

People have an important part to play in developing their own possible selves. It is an experience in the fullest possible exploration of the basic interrelationship between the self and the outer world. People endure great suffering and anguish as they encounter the various losses of life. Their response to these life events will frequently be fashioned and influenced not so much by the size and gravity and frequency of the events, but by the management of the whole constellation of resources currently around them, and those resources not yet explored.

Good planning and preparation can be essential for the effective exercise of those resources. The following seven issues merit serious attention.

Diet

Grief frequently sends its victim in search of comfort and food, and confuses emotional and existential emptiness and hunger with physical emptiness and hunger. If this misconception is fostered, the grieving person is likely to eat excessively or fast excessively, to eat inappropriate foods and not observe regular mealtimes. These practices can lead to problems of size, unhealthy and risk-prone metabolic functioning, high blood pressure and diseases of mismanaged stress, such as diabetes, chronic aches and pains, and digestive disorders.

The life-style of the future requires careful attention to meals, mealtimes, food-intake and diet, reduction of salt and substances high in cholesterol, and maintaining a strong harmony of internal body functioning with body image, identity and the concepts of how a person can be optimally healthy in their bio-social and psychological context.

Physical Fitness

Health and positive coping with stress and adjustment require physical fitness. The person should be encouraged to adopt a regular aerobics exercise program, to avoid risk behaviors, such as erratic and irresponsible driving on the roads, and to refrain from smoking, alcohol overuse and the excessive consumption of other deleterious drugs and substances such as caffeine and salt. They will also be encouraged to observe dental hygiene and to participate in programs related to stress management, self-development and spiritual awareness and enrichment.

While there is widespread recognition that our life-styles are stressful and demanding, we are often reluctant to see that grief and loss reactions are reactions to a particular kind of stress that is often extremely distressing and destructive. Its costs fan out to embrace absenteeism from work, diminished productivity, accident proneness, family disruption and increasing health-related expenses. Change in life-styles can bring a more constructive coping with this stress of loss and grief.

Relaxation and Meditation

Some stressful life-styles call for the introduction of meditation and relaxation training as part of a new life-style. William S. Cohen of the US Senate has said:

> Today, more than ever, the way we die is directly related to the way we live.

Relaxation and meditation may include learning to accept feelings of anxiety, reducing anxiety about anxiety and increasing tolerance for anxiety. People are instructed in the procedures of the daily review (going over the events of the day in reverse without evaluation), affirmation of the positive moments and events of their day, and creating images that engender self-esteem and self-efficacy. Relaxation and meditation are not simply techniques for coping with anxiety and stress. They reflect a different pacing to life, an evolving awareness of a transformation of relationships and of the ecological interweave between the person and the environment, between a way of reacting to events and a life-style where there is a growing consciousness of a participant–observer way of being, of an immediate involvement and the longer view.

Shirley MacLaine (1985) wrote:

"So many people," said Chris, "are moving so swiftly into their understanding of these dimensions. It has changed their lives and the lives of those around them. Their lives are becoming more positive in every way." She looked down at her bare feet. "The world may appear to be in a polarized mess right now, but there are new human beings ready to make a breakthrough. The bell doesn't toll until the time is ready. And the time is now. People are beginning to understand that their spiritual understanding is so much more powerful than their intellectual understanding ..." (p. 319).

During grief and loss reactions we know how we can be frantically preoccupied with what is happening to us. And yet what is happening is not the same as what and who I am. What I know as "me" is separate from my memories, my feelings, my thoughts. Although we search for some meaning to the events of our lives, there is also an intuitive capacity that knows the meaning of things apart from the work of the intellect and the senses. Intuition is to become one with the unified world rather than observing its parts. It is to find the absolute barriers which were accepted as the reality of things, dissolved. It is like listening to music and becoming fully part of that music, letting go and allowing something beyond the style, form and content of the music to become the predominant concern. It is to release the self into a form of meditation and mysticism. It is to relinquish the mode of controlled thinking (with its assembling of information and problem-solving) and possessiveness (with its need to hold on and its fear to let go.) I become and am my awareness. Although we know we have to deal with many of the events in our lives in concrete, practical ways, we come to this other kind of awareness by a discovery, an awakening up, a coming through the trance in which those events seem to hold us.

In grief and loss the person often remarks that he is in a daze, he does not know if it is a dream, that he is only half-awake. Arthur Deikman (1982) wrote:

> When we wake, we know we have been dreaming; while in the dream, there seems to be nothing else (p. 130).

The goal he says is "to awaken fully from the trance of ordinary life." The further we can progress in this regard the more we know a larger reality and a larger self and retrieve that enhancing context of the whole life.

New Tasks

A new life-style will require the development of tasks appropriate to the person, their loss and the social context. Instead of passively awaiting change, the person can be encouraged to be an active and responsive participant in the management of their loss and in the reshaping of a life-style that will reflect that positive management. Judith Wallerstein (1983) gives an example of setting out six psychological tasks for children who have experienced loss through divorce:

1   Acknowledge the reality of the marital rupture and understand the changes that are involved and which are separate from the fantasies that the child will experience.

2   Return to the accepted activities at school and play. This will involve disengaging from the parental conflict and distress despite parental attempts to gain support from the child. It also involves removing the family crisis from its predominant position in the child's thoughts which in turn requires a capacity to control anxiety and depression.

3   Manage and absorb the loss of familiar daily routines, the loss of role, status, house, school, symbols and traditions, and the loss of the protective presence of the two parents and the security of the intactness of the family. This may involve overcoming the sense of rejection, humiliating unlovability and powerlessness that is precipitated by the loss of one parent.

4   Recognize and resolve anger and blame. Unlike bereavement, a divorce is entirely a parental action and decision. Children do not believe in no-fault divorces. They tend to blame one or both parents and sometimes that blame is actively fostered by one parent. The anger can be intense and enduring and has its ongoing effects in other destructive behavior.

5   Accept the permanence of the situation. Children, like some parents, may keep alive the fantasy of returning to a bliss that they had never known. The child of divorce may have greater difficulty accepting the permanence of divorce than the permanence of bereavement.

6   Achieve and sustain a realistic vision of the child's capacity to love and be loved. This is one of the most important tasks for the child and society. It will affect not only the child as he grows up, but also his adulthood and what he transmits to his children.

Similar tasks can be set for other experiences of loss.

Resistance Resources

In effect, people and their environments build up what some have called "psychic capital" (see Sales et al., 1984). They are able to develop life-styles that contribute to ongoing life-styles by stockpiling creative and resistance resources, so that there is greater resilience and psychic capital for meeting future stress and loss.

Life-style

Life-styles place strong emphasis on the environment in which the person has lived, is living and in which they are proposing to live. It is important for us to plan ways to restore pleasure to these environments, to change the mood, tolerance and stimulation of these environments, and to increase the support they provide, and also their positive flow of communication.

From the postures of loss and grief, it is necessary to formulate and plan a creative, happy and holistically oriented life-style. Stresses are converted into problems to be tackled and solved, and meaning and purpose are actively engendered to sustain the will to survive and live fully, until ultimately death itself is faced.

Though outward circumstances change through loss and bereavement, there is a strong need and desire to sustain former life-styles, to regress into fantasies of them and to be preoccupied with attitudes, moods and behavior that reflect dissatisfaction and disillusionment.

There is therefore a need to review regularly the content, direction, mood and tasks of the new life-style, and to confirm its role and status in the important process of restoration.

11

The Place of Religion

God does not die on the day when we cease to believe in a personal
deity, but we die on the day when our lives cease to be illumined by
the steady radiance, renewed daily, of a wonder, the source of which
is beyond all reason.

Dag Hammarskjöld

Growing up as I did in the isolation and loneliness of an
extensive farm in a fairly desolate part of the country, it
was probably inevitable that my first contact with death
would be those of animals and birds. My pathway was to
take me far from that peculiar insularity into the biggest
cities of Europe, Asia and America to meet with people
who were dying, to hear the stories of families whose
loved ones had died or who had been killed in tragic circumstances, and to confer with therapists and counselors
who have gathered together an enormous wisdom to help
mankind's understanding and management of the painful
traumas of loss and death.

As a psychotherapist I have been part of this experience from that particular perspective. As a minister of
religion I have been admitted into other parts of this
public yet intimate turmoil. By virtue of these two roles,
together with a persistent and critical curiosity and ques-
tioning, I have probably seen more of this aspect of

human stress and distress than many other people. I have sat with the distinguished and the decorated in their last hours in the best hospitals in the land, and with an elderly fisherman's wife dying in the poverty of their tiny cottage on the far northeastern coast of Scotland. I have stood with large crowds as parents have buried their child and I have sat with the mother grieving in her isolation for a young soldier for whom there could never be a funeral, for neither his body nor any part of it could be found. I have read drama, story and poem, where death has been defied or denied, and others where the sadness of it all could not be adequately described.

People have traditionally turned to religion at times of death and grief. There we witness a wide range of attempted systematization of beliefs, experiences, rituals and behavior — from the restrained intellectualization of death to mystical experiences, to the wild frenzy of emotion and religious fervor. There is so much apparent paradox involved that it is difficult to know what is authentic or healthy or justifiable.

One family deeply attached to their father decided on a private funeral with a simple announcement in the newspaper two days later. Another family who had had a very conflicting and anxious relationship with their father held a large public funeral; not surprisingly the family squabbled over every aspect of the church service and had a bitter argument an hour after the colorful ceremonial service was concluded.

I have been a little amused (if that is not too indecorous a word) to witness the funeral of an archbishop attended by hundreds of bishops and clergy and the so-called ordinary faithful people. They gave him an ornate mass and then interred his body in the crypt of the cathedral. The man had been afforded at his death the highest honor the Church could bestow on the dead body of one of its illustrious servants; yet most knew that in many of his dealings with them, and in several of the schemes he had developed, he had shown he could be a scoundrel.

We have seen prime ministers and eminent politicians buried or cremated, their bodies treated to the last moment as if they were something more than what they were. Often I have wondered why such public occasions are so acclaimed, when the thousands of men and women killed in wars to which these other people committed them received no funeral at all.

In more recent times there has been a great deal of rethinking about the part religion and the churches should play at times of death and in providing the funeral ceremony. This rethinking has been part of a wider reappraisal of religion and church in our culture. Funerals have moved from the churches to funeral homes, to the crematorium or graveside, and the person speaking the words might be male or female, clergy or nonclergy. The involvement of nonclerical civil celebrants has become a popular practice, particularly in the large cities. It is interesting to see that many civil celebrants retain many of the traditional religious forms and adopt similar roles. Some have read widely about grief and their words reflect the current literature that has impressed them most; others listen to the mourners and tend to use words that give expression to a diffuse emotionality and purging. Overall, it can be a thoughtful departure from the stereotyping of word, style and role of the conventional clergy presentation. Curiously, although some clergy claim that they have moved away from these stereotypes, observers believe they still hear more of the same.

Religion has probably always drawn ambivalent reactions and behavior from its followers. On the one hand religion has always been in the business of bargaining with the secular powers, making decisions about people's lives and jobs, buying and selling property, attempting to instill fear and enforce behavior. On the other hand religion has always been seen as some kind of bridge between this life and some other life, between "this world and the next," between man and God.

The word religion means to bind. Primitively and conventionally that binding has been interpreted as binding man to God and binding man's behavior and belief. This kind of binding has taken precedence over the goals of religion which have been:

- to bind man to high ideals and to great dreams of a better humanity;
- to bind man to life and all life's affirmations;
- to bind men and women together in equality and peace; and
- to bind the human community in the cause of a new creation.

Some religions, instead of bringing men and women into the mystery and wonder of creation and life's possibilities, have become rather prosaic and predictable, and not too mysterious. These forms of religion are preoccupied with the sinful nature of man, the threat of damnation and the need to be bound by tyrannous beliefs and rules. Religion's function is often perceived as some kind of bridge to get us into the next life. Little heed is given to the words of Rabia, the Sufi saint, quoted by Arthur Deikman (1982):

O Lord –
If I worship ... you from the fear of
hell, cast me into hell;

If I worship ... you from the desire for
paradise, deny me paradise (p. 117).

Particularly at times of death, we see what forms religion comes to take. Here it has to deal with the body of an individual and the meaning the survivors give to the body and to the future. It has to deal with attachments and loss, with memories and attributions, with the realities of death and the way it is possible to go on living.

In their highest moments, Judeo–Christian religions have emphasized these major themes:

- affirming life, and living it fully;
- expressing an ultimate concern;
- listening to the depths of experience;
- moving toward a oneness with God;
- celebrating a resurrection and the symbols of a new life or new creation; and
- grasping the courage to be and to live meaningfully with others.

There have of course been other major themes of religion that emphasized:

- man's sinful nature and need of repentance;
- rules and beliefs necessary for salvation;
- punishment in this life and the next;
- favors in this life and the next;
- the individual's personal responsibility, piety and salvation; and
- the assurance of life after death for those who have proved their worth, and a great deal of anxiety for those who were not certain.

There is little wonder that many people in our contemporary society are confused by the teaching of religion and the churches on matters of loss and death. There are two extreme positions.

At one extreme there is the fundamentalist position. It is attractive in its unequivocal teaching, its literal interpretation of the Bible, its assertion of an imposed authority, and it is persuasive in the numbers that adhere to it. Its view is emphatically of a personal pursuit of piety and salvation with the assurance of life after death. The other extreme is the affirmative position which affirms that life is to be lived fully here and now, that the oneness of life with God is a communal-ecological-interdependent oneness, and that God gives to people the unfolding capacities to participate in life and to affirm continuously its possibilities in the here-and-now. It affirms that the past can be left with God, the future is with God, and the present is given in grace to us.

Some people would see themselves between these two extremes, but most are religiously illiterate and confused and are easy targets of others' persuasion and emotional blackmail. Regressive tendencies are readily induced. It is not surprising that people veer away from actualizing the fullness of life in the present, to accept the sentiments of pie in the sky when you die.

William James (1842–1910), once described as America's greatest psychologist, advocated:

- that the visible world in which we live each day is part of a more spiritual universe from which it draws its significance;
- that a harmonious relation with that higher universe is our goal and the direction in which we should travel;
- that a communion with the Spirit of that other uni-

verse is possible and thereby spiritual energy flows in and produces effects, psychological and material, within the visible world of our experience; and

- that we can experience a union with something beyond, and larger than, ourselves, that is friendly to us and our ideals, and in that union we can find our greatest peace. (See Knight, 1950, p. 217.)

Within the various religions specific people have emphasized particular components of the religious, mystical and God–man relationships, and some have claimed to be emissaries of the higher Spirit charged and gifted with the task of revelation and liberation. In the Christian religion Jesus was such a person and he in turn gathered the assistance of a small band of disciples and followers, some of whom became the writers of the gospels and letters collected in the New Testament.

It was not surprising that the quest for union with the Spirit of this and another universe should also find the prospect of immortality and life after death in some of the teachings of religious founders. The notion is comforting to some and alarming to others; a logical sequence to some and nonsense to others. When we examine the teaching of Jesus, there are those who see that the predominant teaching and the key to his mission were summed up in the words "I have come that men may have life, and may have it in all its fullness" (John 10:10). The clear implication was a here-and-now fulfillment. Others have seen that the main thrust of his mission was to point people to the possibility of life in another realm after this life. In the same gospel (John 14:2), he says:

There are many dwelling places in my Father's house; if it were not so I should have told you; for I am going there on purpose to prepare a place for you.

If we add to such words the various references to a promise of eternal life, the argument for immortality seems to become firmer.

Two issues, at least, complicate this argument. The first is that Jesus was not only a teacher but a mystic and we in the Western world have difficulty with that. When Jesus said that he was one with the Father and that he prayed that we might be one, our Western tendency is to convert that into a physical literalism. When he spoke of eternal life, our tendency is to interpret that in chronological or linear terms, so that it comes to mean literally life never-ending. But the words "eternal life" referred not to the length dimension of life, but to its depth and quality and to the victory of courage in the struggle with conflict, ambiguity and tragedy. One of the outstanding theologians of the century, Paul Tillich (1964), wrote of the concept of immortality:

> In some Protestant countries it has become the last remnant of the whole Christian message, but it has done so in the non-Christian pseudo-Platonic form of a continuation of the temporal life of an individual after death without a body. Where the symbol of immortality is used to express this popular superstition, it must be radically rejected by Christianity; for participation in eternity is not "life hereafter". Neither is it a natural quality of the human soul. It is rather the creative act of God, who lets the temporal separate itself from and return to the eternal (p. 437).

When St. Paul (1 Corinthians 15:53) speaks of that transformation when "what is mortal must be clothed with immortality," he does not mean that we thus cease to be finite, but that — finite as we are — we are absorbed or taken into the infinite, the eternal.

Eternal life is to be seen then as life in the eternal, life in God. To be "in" God means three things:

- that its origins arise from God;
- that its capacity to exist comes from God; and
- that its direction and fulfillment are in that context of God.

This theological view holds that God draws everything toward this fulfillment of the Divine Life itself and this is the content of divine blessedness. This is not a state of immortality or perfection, but a state of participating in, and being grasped by, the Divine Spirit while simultaneously participating in the negative aspects of our existence and the ambiguities of life.

The quest for some assurance of survival for the self is not limited to religion and theology. Yale University's professor of psychiatry, Robert Lifton (1973), wrote:

The need to transcend death ... represents a compelling urge to maintain an inner sense of continuous symbolic relationship, over time and space, with the various elements of life. In other words, I am speaking of a *sense* of immortality as in itself neither compensatory nor pathological, but as man's symbolization of his ties with both his biological fellows and his history, past and future (p. 6).

Lifton proposed that this sense of immortality was expressed in five modes:

1 The biological mode, which becomes meaningful in the sense of living on through one's children and their children, through one's students and perhaps their colleagues
2 The theological mode
3 The "works" mode, found in the sense that one lives on through one's achievements, writings, influences and words

4   The theme of nature, that our immortality is found in the endless seasons and rhythms of nature

5   The mode of transcendence, experienced as "losing oneself," the achievement of ecstasy and rapture, psychic unity and perceptual intensity.

Most people have little difficulty recognizing some aspects of their diffuse quest for this sense of immortality in these five modes. We run into controversy with the theological mode, particularly in some expressions of Christian teaching and dogmatism about the "life here-after." From time to time I have stated that this was not a basic Christian belief, but that it has become a distor-tion and a misinterpretation of Christian language and teaching. It was a reversion to a sub-Christian notion of a duality of body and spirit contradicting the Christian concept of Spirit which includes all dimensions of being. From an experiential point of view I am prepared to be agnostic about life hereafter. We simply do not know what happens to the human spirit and personality. We do know that for a time that personality is remembered, but with the passing of time and more than one generation, it is forgotten although a name persists on the family tree as a symbol of a person who once lived.

There is the other problem of sheer comprehension: how can we talk of life after death when the two words stand as direct opposites? A person who is living is not dead, and a person who is dead cannot be regarded as living. There are peculiarities of language and definition that sometimes might confuse the issue: we talk about people being "half dead" or "nearly dead" or that "he might as well be dead." We say that this one is not "legally dead" whereas that one is "emotionally (or psychologi-cally) dead" or "spiritually dead." There are also the

boundary-line definitions of determining the point of
death medically, legally and functionally.

This confusion was highlighted in Koko's words in the
last act of *The Mikado*:

> It's like this. When Your Majesty says, "let a thing be done",
> it's as good as done — practically it is done ... Your Majesty
> says, "Kill a gentleman", and a gentleman is taken off to be
> killed! Consequently that gentleman is as good as dead —
> practically he is dead — and if he is dead, why not say so?

12

The Final Observances

I don't know why I walked out toward the orchard. All the work there was done. But I guess I had to give a goodnight to Papa, and be alone with him. The bugs were out, and their singing was all around me. Almost like a choir. I got to the fresh grave, all neatly mounded and pounded. Somewhere down under all that Vermont clay was my father, Haven Peck. Buried deep in the land he sweated so hard on and longed to own so much. And now it owned him. "Good night, Papa," I said. "We had thirteen good years."

That was all I could say, so I just turned and walked away from a patch of grassless land.

Robert Newton Peck

When a person dies, the family, or those vested with responsibility, must give their early attention to the burial or the cremation. This is a hygenic necessity as well as a cultural practice dating back, according to archeological findings, to Neanderthal man of the Middle Paleolithic period. In our culture there are wide varieties of practice for carrying out this essential task of appropriately removing the body to the place of burial or cremation. We have traditionally interwoven into that basic task some of the rituals of mourning and commemoration. It may be helpful if we now comment upon some of those final observances which will contribute to the recovery from grief and affirm the salient processes of life.

I include a discussion of practices that could be included in a service of burial or cremation. It reflects a Christian baseline, as this is the form in which I have had

198 · Life After Loss

most experience. Anyone attending a funeral service in a Christian church will see such differences of practice that it is hardly believable that this is a common religion. On the one hand there are the rituals of a Requiem Mass; on the other hand there is the starkly simple unadorned graveside committal with an extempore prayer and a Bible reading by a minister of church or sect that observes no ceremony and uses no symbol or robe of office. I have been to services where exactly the same readings and prayers are read regardless of the circumstances of the death or the beliefs and religious involvements of the immediate family and friends.

Churches and clergy can be so committed to their customs that they apparently disregard the fact that the words, language and form of the service are incomprehensible to the listeners, and that most of them are not listening anyway. I have seen clergy zealously reading the set prayers, or others engaged in some kind of private and linguistically esoteric conversation with God, while the congregation has shown little interest or comprehension. Often the mourners will be more affected by the attitude and empathy of the clergy than by the ritual that the mourners perceive the clergy are bound to follow. Whatever is said and done at the funeral could be part of the adaptation process; unfortunately, this is not often the case. It would be better if clergy locked away their prayer books and sat down to spend some time to think through what effective role they could play in the recovery and ultimate health and well-being of the mourners. They would then be in a position to write a relevant service for each situation. Regretfully, I believe this goal will not be widely followed, chiefly I suspect, for two reasons.

The first is that clergy are more preoccupied with protecting their own role of being carriers of the gospel than they are with the needs and ultimate health and well-being of the mourners. Many of course would dispute this, saying that the preaching of the gospel and the ultimate health of the people are inseparable. We are soon involved therefore in the conflict between a deductive approach, where the clergy bring their resources to the grief situation, and the inductive situation where they, first of all, listen to the grief situation to hear its questions, peculiarities and needs.

The second reason is that clergy are generally untrained for the vital task of being part of the mourners' rehabilitation process. They are generally inequipped to be creative and inductive in these situations and it can be so much easier to turn to the prescribed forms. It must be said that the prescribed forms, though often lacking relevance to the situation, are to be preferred to some of the ramblings and unempathic and unintelligent statements I have heard at some funerals.

At one funeral the gathered congregation were in a mood of gratitude and inspiration — they had been ennobled in themselves and elevated in their dignity to be part of a humanity which had been graced by the man who had died. He had gone through great suffering and died with courage that had touched them all. How incongruous that the minister in solemn voice should begin the service with the prayer that asked that we (the congregation) might "be lifted above our darkness and distress." What darkness? What distress?

At another service the congregation had gathered with the family for the funeral of an 88-year-old grandmother. For nine years she had been a heavy nursing burden. She was a large woman: she had a stroke which resulted in a paralysis of her right side and she moved in and out of senile confusion. Prior to her stroke at the age of 79, she

had lived with her married daughter and her husband and
family for twenty-two years. It was an enormous relief
when she died. The minister prayed and read and talked
interminably, so it seemed. He spoke about the sufferings
of life and the promises of the afterlife, but at no stage
identified with the family reaction. As this service came
gradually to its end, his voice became quieter, until at
length he paused, then whispered, "Let us go unto the
cemetery." Even his words seemed to indicate he was in
another world, but he so misjudged his listeners that a
large section of them struggled to restrain their impulse of
laughter.

During the course of one seminar on grief which I
attended, I heard a distinguished professor of pastoral care
instruct his students (all training for the ministry) that
they should start their funeral service with words that
reflected where the people were. He told them to start by
saying "We are here in the presence of death." In my
opinion he was wrong. He was wrong because it is not a
presence, it is a state or a word used to describe a state.
Why say "We are here in the presence of death" when we
do not say "We are here in the presence of life"? He was
also wrong because he was making his first statement his
preoccupation with the negative and possibly the
inexplicable, when he might better have affirmed a few
known positives.

At the funeral of a young man killed in an industrial
accident I heard a minister giving the professor's injunc-
tion some expression, although I am sure he had never
heard the professor to whom I have alluded. Anxious to
make some contact with a large young audience all of
whom looked unchurched, he began by saying, "Now this
is a pretty tricky situation we are in today ... I don't know
what to say that would make any sense to you as to why

this young fellow is dead today." The fact was, every one of those young people knew why he was dead. He made a fatal error, was dragged into a machine which decollated him before anyone had seen what had happened. Perhaps their question was not so much "Why is he dead?" but "How will we live now?"

The funeral is a very small event in the whole upheaval of loss and grief. In recent times funeral directors, involved in the competition of company survival as well as being service providers, are tending to make far more out of the funeral than they once did. Media coverage of some funerals adds to this competitive and communal need for a recognizable and distinctive performance. But we should not for a moment be persuaded into thinking that the funeral has very much positive value for the relief of grief. It can accentuate grief and sometimes it encourages a wallowing in it.

I have seen funerals where the family's need to grieve has been confused with their desire to make a public statement. Some funerals and memorial services can express a public appreciation and even a sense of grandeur that someone in their living and dying has been and done something of significance in enhancing their own and the wider humanity. But this needs to be distinguished from the excessive spending and public show which seem to some people to be the way to express their grief, or their way of demonstrating something to their community. In some instances the luxury funeral has been a compensation for the deprived life, a way of maintaining a public recognition and perception even where there has been an improverished private experience.

Funerals frequently reveal how preoccupied we are with the human body, and what difficulty we have in coping with its loss. An excessive materialism joins with a powerful body-concern to preclude people from coming to terms with what is actually occurring. They spare no cost, insist on excessive procedures, for they have a love to express, and how can that occur except through their attachment to the body? They want to do something for the one who has died, but there is also a concealed denial that the person has died and they act as if death had not really occurred. Behind these activities there is a primitive fear, belief or half-belief, that the one who has died is witnessing the whole event and may be capable of a punitive or revengeful return.

It is important to recognize that funerals have a basic task plus some form of ceremony. Many people choose to have no ceremony. Others have the ceremony without the basic task (perhaps the body was lost at sea or destroyed in an air disaster). Others again have neither task nor ceremony. The speed of recovery and relief from their mourning is rarely dependent on, or affected by, the actual funeral ceremony. Many regularly say that certain aspects of the ceremony and certain people were especially helpful, gratifying, encouraging and inspiring — even where an observer might have wondered how it could have possibly been so. Although these appreciative remarks may be reflecting some significant experience of that moment, they may not have much significance for the important task of relief of inner pain and the recovery from grief, which may need to take place in a different context.

A funeral itself may have five distinct parts, with content modified for each particular ceremony. Its form will reflect the tradition of the minister or the people of a given situation. But this five-part ceremony focuses on:

- the task;

- life and death;
- the person who has died;
- the mourners; and
- reaffirmation of the task.

The Task

People go to a funeral to perform certain tasks, though they may never have articulated what the tasks are to be. These may be expressive, participatory, vicarious, religious, representational, performance or obligatory tasks. The clergy or officiating person may have tasks that are performance, controlling, caring and religious tasks. Some clergy believe their job is to say the rite, to perform the ritual and ceremony set down by the church. Some may see that their task is to care for people in their distress and grief, to find ways to bring control and serenity to a turbulent situation, to set people on a pathway of reinterpreting their experience and to help them take some steps toward a positive adaptation to the reality of life's events and the formation of a new life-style.

The basic tasks often become concealed by other needs and concerns; they can easily become lost under the superstructure of words and ceremony, or the pretensions of piety and sentiment.

The basic task is the recognition of the death of a person, the removal of the body and the restructuring of life without that person being present ever again.

People gather together because they have heard of the death of "David Llewellyn." Their first task is to gather together. They want to express their individual and corporate tribute. They may feel some gratitude for having known him and for what he was, and their task is to proclaim that gratitude. They have a task of assuring each other, and those who mourn him most, of their support, and of the importance of having the courage to be and go on, in spite of anxiety, ambiguity and tragedy.

Thus these tasks might be expressed: "We gather together at a time like this to express our tributes — our own specific tribute and the tribute of all of us together — to 'David Llewellyn' who has been a part of our lives in many ways and at differing depths. We have gratitude that we would like to express to him, gratitude to life in which we all shared, and gratitude to God who is the source and energy of all life. We also gather to express our concern and support for those of his closest circle — family, friends and colleagues — that they may find that strength and courage will rise out of the ongoing flow of life, out of our concern for them and out of our common life in God."

Life and Death

Here we might give expression to three anxieties and three affirmations. There is the ontological dread of our collision with the ever-present threat that hangs over being: the threat of nonbeing; the collision with our common finitude. There is the anxiety that pertains to the particular death of "David Llewellyn" — its meaninglessness, its ambiguity, its paradox. And there is the anxiety of "where to from here" — the anxiety of succumbing to an unlived life, and the anxiety of not knowing how to respond to the new claims that life makes upon us.

The affirmations are likewise threefold. There is the affirmation that life and death are part of the source and ground of all being; that we are one scene in the larger play; that we are part of an ongoing process. Secondly, there is the affirmation that as people, even in their despair, search the depths, there emerges a new perspective, a new courage and a new reassurance that they can place meaning on the meaningless. Though they are constrained by the boundaries, the boundaries can be redrawn; a person can "remap his soul and find in it territories he never thought possible, attainable or even desirable" (Wilber, 1979). Thirdly, there is the affirmation that life is our task and its renewal and fulfillment our goal. We are, as St. Paul said:

> Hard-pressed on every side, we are never hemmed in; bewildered, we are never at our wits' end; hunted, we are never abandoned to our fate; struck down, we are not left to die (2 Corinthians 4:8–9).

He was indicating that though we experience an existential alienation, we are never far from the presence of the One who is ultimately the source of life and courage. Although we lose someone to whom we were deeply attached, yet there is a "something" that calls us out of ourselves and our submission to death and inauthenticity to experience in discovery and grace a new awareness of that oneness.

These affirmations may be expressed in:

- form;
- behavior;
- word; and
- ceremony.

The *form* involves the place and symbols. The church building — from small country structure to the large ornate cathedral — has a powerful symbolism. It links a small group with the vast family of the world, this moment in time with the searching of the centuries, this isolated event with the eternal grace of God. The church's external shape points us toward the elevation of the human spirit and transcendence of the human circumstance. Its internal furnishings and symbols remind us of the various ways men and women have struggled to understand the mysteries and suffering of life, and the many ways the Divine Spirit has revealed or opened the ways for courage and healing, wholeness and hope. In similar ways the form of the ceremony and the priestly or ministerial vestments all have a capacity to communicate the power of a symbol that joins mankind in a long procession, that speaks of a joining of worlds, that reflects both the ordinariness of our humanity and the cloaks of a different humanity touching the promise of eternal blessedness.

To a growing extent, people feel so estranged from church and clergy and from the symbols and their meaning that funerals take place at the funeral home. Many funeral directors have gone to great care to provide places of solace and, in some cases, substitute places for the church. But in the sense of which I have been speaking they can never be a substitute. They are not places where people through the years have worshipped, there is no altar for the sacrament of holy communion and the music is often an attempt to bring a maudlin religion into a nonreligious place. It would be far more inspiring to play the recorded music of parts of Beethoven's Sixth or Ninth Symphony or C. H. H. Parry's "Jerusalem" (better known as the stirring theme of the film *Chariots of Fire*) than attempting to provide a canned version of "Abide with me" or "Rock of Ages." Similarly, the chapels of the crematorium are once again attempts at church imitation.

When there is such scope for ceremonies in buildings that could be opened by better use of glass to the gardens and flowers, it is such an oppressive experience to be brought into such heavy-walled structures that communicate the narrow tunnel of one's last journey.

Country cemeteries have such a significant mood for me that I wonder why people do not use a cemetery service on its own rather than a church or funeral home setting. In the graveyard you have gathered around all the indications of man's finitude and mortality, but you also have the symbols of sky, cloud and bird, earth, grass and flower — and the wind: "The wind passeth over it and it is gone and the place thereof shall know it no more" (Psalm 103:16).

A common practice in the larger cities is for a service to be held in the church or funeral home, followed by a long, tedious and strained journey to the crematorium where another briefer service for committal is held. Many families have come to feel (or by common practice have been persuaded to feel) that this is the appropriate form of making a last tribute and saying a final farewell. In country places the funeral procession of cars still holds considerable significance and has a unique way of reminding everyone of their mortality and final pathway. But in large cities where traffic and distance compete against all expressions of dignity and reverence, these practices are harder to sustain in any meaningful way.

The central figures of the drama always give a final significance to the occasion. I have seen large funeral processions which have been large in form with little feeling, and others where there has been high emphasis on the feeling and little regard for form. At the other end of the spectrum I have seen a handful of people stand around a grave and give the occasion far more dignity and significance than some large ceremonial funerals. But I have also seen another handful of people feeling under obligation to be there, ready to race away before they have time to note why they have come or the nature of their common mortality.

For a form of funeral, I commend three practices:

1 Hold a gathering-together at the church. This can be done with the casket present, or can be held as the cremation is taking place. There is also the possibility of holding the public gathering at one time, and a private cremation or burial at another time, or at the discretion of the funeral director.

2 Hold the one service at the crematorium or the cemetery.

3 Arrange for some appropriate gathering-together after the service or after the funeral — where other expressions and tributes can be made and where there is the usual ample opportunity for some emotional healing and acceptance of the new reality through social interchange and support.

Behavior at funerals can be fraught with uncertainty and anxiety. For everyone, there is the decision to be there and to accept one's being there. There are behaviors for those who are in the closer group and family of the mourners, and there are behaviors for all those attending. The family mourners might go through the procedure in detail with the person conducting the service; ask every possible question of where to meet, where to sit, where to stand, when to move, what to do at the end of the service, where to go, what to say. Rehearse in word and imagery before the event. Likewise the person conducting the service should take the most detailed care to traverse beforehand with each of the family mourners, the steps of the service, the points of involvement, what the mourners might say and how they might act.

And let there be an abundance of flowers. It reflects a misconception when people place notices in the bereavement columns of the newspapers saying "No flowers by request." On the contrary, the notice should read "Send a ton of flowers, by special request." Do not send wreaths that are carted to the cemetery or crematorium, displayed for a few minutes, then picked up on a front-end loader and dumped or simply left in the weather to wither and die. No, send bowls of flowers, bunches and bouquets, sheafs and posies — and send them in all their color and fragrance. Flowers remind us of the great and wonderful spirit of creation, of nature, of the ever-returning seasons. They speak their memorable message that in times of sadness and grayness, there can be a magnificent splash of color. Send plenty of flowers so that everyone can take a bunch home with them, that in the commemoration of a death, we also carried away a reminder of the affirmation of life.

The *words* that are used may not be remembered, but the way they are said will be valued. People expressing their sympathy and support can do so in a firm and simple sentence. Do not overstress the mourner by long statements. Your presence is the first affirmation. Shake hands, or, if appropriate, gently embrace the person and say something simple.

"I am pleased I am with you today."

"I have been thinking of you."

"She was an important influence in my life."

"She was an outstanding person."

"We were good friends."

"We were proud to be part of her life."

The mourners need say very little. "Thank you" ... "We are sad, but you being here gives us a little more strength" ... "Thank you for coming" ... "Thank you for being such a person to her." All statements reflect important affirmations.

The words used by the person conducting the service to convey the affirmations will usually be of three categories.

The first would be *statements of general perspective,* such as the following:

"At times when someone close to us dies we are immediately concerned with what has happened to them, and how their dying affects us in so many different ways. We know that death is not an isolated event. Before a death there has been life and that life has had many special and unique characteristics. In dying and death we all come face to face with the peculiar paradox of life and death: that we are all part of this ongoing process, and that in all our living and dying, life continues. For a time we each share in the life process, then leave it, and others follow on."

"Those of religious faith can take strength and courage from the struggle of men and women of faith through the centuries, that in their quest for the meaning of life and death, they discovered something that could be passed on to future generations and to us; they also believed that their God was a God of all life — its source, its strength, its end ... and as they in their various ways came closer to him, they found strength and courage to live and die ... knowing that although they suffered and died, he was always with them and they were always with him ... such was his love and concern for all his creation."

"We also have the words of Jesus who claimed a special closeness to that Eternal Father. He reassured us and reconfirmed that basic belief that the Fatherhood of God transcended the finite boundaries of the life and death of each person … and that living or dying, we all can be part of the One and the Oneness of God and Life and Creation."

The second category of affirmation would be the *readings from the Scriptures*. Various readings are set down in the prayer books for such occasions. My preferences are as follows, though only one or two would be used on a given occasion:

Deuteronomy 34:1–6	Moses looks on the promised land in all its excellence: it was worth the struggle, though he was not to live long enough to enter it.
Ruth 1:15–19	Ruth reassures Naomi that "where you go I will go."
Job 12:10–16	Job recalls that in God's hand are the souls of all that live.
Job 22:21–26	Job's friend tells Job to come to terms with God.
Job 28:12–15, 20–28	Job contemplates where wisdom might be found.

Psalm 23; 27:1–6; 40:42–43; 46; 62; 67; 90; 103; 107:1–15; 121

Ecclesiastes 3:1–11	A contemplation of the various times in life.
Isaiah 40:1–11	A great statement of comfort and hope.
Isaiah 40:21–31	An affirmation about God and the strength he gives.
Daniel 12:5–12	A reassurance for the end of the age.
Habakkuk 3:15–19	In spite of everything, a faith prevails.
Matthew 5:1–16	The Beatitudes.
John 6:14–21	The symbol of Jesus stilling the storm.
John 10:7–14	Jesus speaks of his basic care and his concern for life in all its fullness.
John 14:1–7	Jesus speaks of trust and courage.
John 20:13–17	Jesus tells Mary not to cling to him but to spread the word of new life.
Romans 5:1–5	God's love has flooded our whole being.
Romans 8:18–39	The whole created universe groaning. Nothing separates us from the love of God.
1 Corinthians 2:6–12	Things prepared by God for all who love him.

2 Corinthians 4:7–18	We are inwardly renewed.
Ephesians 2:13–22	You who were once far off have been brought near.
Colossians 1:9–20	May he strengthen you.
Colossians 2:6–8	Be built in him.
Colossians 3:12–16	Let Christ's peace be arbiter in your hearts.
Hebrews 12:1–2	Run with resolution the race for which we are entered.
1 Peter 1:3–7	A great affirmation.
Revelation 21:1–5	A vision of reassurance.

The third category includes other readings: *poems, affirmations, stories of relevance.* Some excellent readings could be drawn from the following:

Kahlil Gibran: *The Prophet*
Rabindranath Tagore: *Collected Poems and Plays*
Nikos Kazantzakis: *Report to Greco*
J. Krishnamurti: *The First and Last Freedom*
Marjorie Pizer: *Selected Poems 1963–1983*
Paul Tillich: *The Courage to Be*

The *ceremony* reveals a great deal about the affirmations we have to declare. I have been to many funerals. A large portion of them clearly emphasize the ceremony of death, sorrow, slowness, emptiness, mourning. A further large proportion have no ceremony that anyone could notice. The presiding person reflects — in posture, movement and word — their anxiety, desire to please or need to do what is necessary and leave. There is little presence and even less presentation.

A funeral is an important milestone in people's lives. This is not stage, but real drama. It is true that many present are often accused of hypocrisy and double-talk, but even that is part of the real drama of human relationships and the human moments of living and dying. The ceremony includes people, movement toward each other and movement away from each other; it brings the past into the present, it includes music, the spoken word and a presence that memorably portray something significant about the human community and something stabilizing and stengthening to each human soul.

The Person Who Has Died

Many people gather at funerals because they can be notable social occasions, a source of anecdote and conversation for weeks afterwards. But an essential focus must be the person who has died.

The death may have been traumatic and tragic, or it may have been expected and welcomed. The focus may be a young child, a young woman, a father of a young family, an elderly lady like my aunt who was wishing her death would hurry in its coming. The person's life may have not really established a direction; it may be in its mid-life peak or flourish. The person may have distinguished himself in his work, or been a special and significant person to several groups. Or it could be the person lived an apparently empty existence; he was boring and colorless, or perhaps he did so very little that even simple remarks seem like exaggerations.

Whether we are speaking of the distinguished or the

dull, the very young or the elderly, all have been given the gift of life. All have been touched by this grace. For a moment all hostilities and demands cease, all claims about rights and privileges, all the striving for the next goal are quietened — while we stand to contemplate the mystery and generosity of Life giving life and then receiving life back to Life, and all of it part of the paroxysm and process of grace. Nobody can demand to be born. Nobody can bargain their birth. Nobody can say they knew beforehand that they were worthy of life. Yet it happened. It was given. It was grace. Thus in speaking of the person who has died we speak of this grace.

We can go further, for life comes and goes regardless of our worth or even our ability to accept it and make something of it. Some people make a great deal of it but it seems it is too hurriedly snatched from them. Others make nothing of it over a long lifetime — life seems factitious, unappreciated and misappropriated. But always grace says, regardless of the brevity or length of life, "Life receives its own." In spite of our unacceptability in one or many ways, we are accepted.

To pay our tribute to the one who has died, we say this is who they were — a unique identity, sharing in life and being touched by grace. Here and there, or maybe in some remarkable ways, we saw that grace shine in them and we were affected by the joyful glory of it. But in some, we see little sign of grace being recognized; yet we know that life being given, grace was also there. This we affirm and celebrate.

The Mourner

A mourner's pathway is not an easy one and it is heavily

loaded with resistance and relief, with unmistakable pain and with confusing contradictions. Another mourner's pathway is accepted as a matter of course, while some feel they must conceal their sense of freedom and release.

A 62-year-old woman said at the gathering for tea and cake after the funeral of her husband: "Well, Bernie's gone, and I can tell you I'm not a bit sorry. It may sound to you as if I have no feelings, but I think he's better off where he is. Life was always a bother to him and he became so tiresome to us all. No, I've got to be honest. I've waited a long time to feel as I do today."

On the other hand a 27-year-old man was devastated by the death of his wife on the second day of their honeymoon. He was not only distressed for himself, but kept returning to his inconsolable sorrow for his wife. "She was so full of every expectation. Now she can never have it. She was such a beautiful person. Whenever I was without her, my mind was full of the images of her softness and gentleness. Now she can't have that and be that any more. We'd often said that so many people walk around as if they have the artificial support system on 'low.' She was just the opposite; full of vitality and joy. Now — nothing. I can't bear it."

The mourners feel that a bond has been broken and that something which was once close to them, if not part of their possession then part of their life space, has been placed outside their reach, their control and their ongoing interaction. Thus the channels of expectation or frustration, of attachment and entanglement, have suddenly been disrupted. Mourners may have two simultaneous reactions — one for themselves and the other for the dead person; one of pain or relief in the self, the other the pain or relief of the dead person. The mourner, being the survivor, is host to both feelings. Although it often seems as if they can attribute feeling to the dead person, the feelings are within them. Some people find it difficult to release themselves; indeed a resistance tends to keep them there as a way of sustaining some continuing contact with the dead person. Others are uncertain about what to do with their feelings. We are ready to accommodate the wide range of verbalizations and behavior that may reflect this uncertainty and its mixture of frustration and anger, helplessness and despair; or liberation and freedom, revenge and determination.

From what has been said in early chapters, we know that the mourners, whatever the circumstances of the death, will undergo many changes in the several areas of their lives: their feelings, their thinking, their inner mind, their behavior and life-style. They will make their efforts to apprehend the meaning of the event by which they have been grasped, and in their lives they will reflect their efforts to shape that event.

The 27-year-old man whose wife was killed on their honeymoon examined the events of her death repeatedly. He said, "I concluded it was one of those strange flukes of life, totally meaningless in itself and a shocking waste. But once I saw what it was, and that it was a reality, I knew I had to start walking again."

His second marriage ended in divorce after six years. His third marriage, now in its twelfth year, is stable and very satisfactory.

The funeral can be part of the process whereby the mourner recognizes the reality of the death; that meaning must be given to life and death; that a reorganization has to take place, and that the process has already begun.

Funerals have always been occasions for gathering people together. We often fail to appreciate the potential value of this gathering-together. I know that mourners are often helped most of all at funerals by the simple awareness that so many people attended. People who have gathered are understandably uncertain about their role, anxious about funerals and sensitive about the feelings of those most intimately affected by the death. There is a tendency to huddle in small groups or to come and go as quickly as possible.

Only relatively recently have we begun to articulate what experientially and intuitively we have known for generations: that we cope better with our stresses if we have effective support groups and networks around us; that our coping is more likely to be adaptive if we perceive that our supportive influences are being supportive. Support groups can give people:

- a bond of belonging, identity, trust and care;
- a sense of shared involvement, motivation and hope;
- a sense of self-confidence, enhancement and purpose;
- a different perspective, another assessment of the situation, the available resources, the processes of setting and reaching goals; and
- supplies of various resources from food to guidance, from equipment to skills. (See Macnab, 1985, pp. 343–4.)

Funerals, in form and content, can focus on the value of support, and in some instances, encouragement may be given as to the ways in which that support might be acceptably and appropriately actualized.

Loss and death make many subtle incursions into one's sense of worth, identity, self-confidence and self-efficacy. The effects of this can be unsettling to those who have been overtly and materially dependent or emotionally and in fantasy attached to the person who died.

"I feel shattered."
"I just fell to pieces."
"I don't know who I am anymore."
"I feel as if I'm nobody and nobody cares."
Walter Bonime (1981) wrote:

Functional ineffectiveness is a frightening event because it is a subjective perception that: What is ME doesn't work (p. 89).

Funerals can reaffirm the autonomy and the interdependence of people within their caring communities. They can remind people of their sense of who they are in their own right and status, and they can endorse the worth and the integrity of the self in spite of tragedy and loss and their unsettling anxiety. The person with a strong sense of self is more likely to cope with stress than the person with a fragmented sense of self or low self-esteem. From positive self-worth we can then develop self-assertion, self-activity and self-skills.

Positive self-worth does not place a person above the anxieties of existence but it does provide an important undergirding for flexibly tolerating and managing the uncertainty and anxiety. This does not mean that the person is, or can be, an isolate in the human situation. At times they will feel as if they are more than an isolate: they are actually targeted by fate. The need to withdraw within one's boundaries or to draw higher protections around those boundaries can be very strong.

Mourners are to be encouraged persistently to rediscover their personal contact with their environment and so become free of that resistance and those devices that at the cost of so much pain seem to be necessary for living.

The funeral can be a symbol — positive and mobile — of the mourner's specific individuality and the respect for their way of being. At the same time it is a symbol of their movement toward being part of all Being; toward the crossing of hitherto inflexible boundaries; toward the discovery of that oneness of the web of life; toward becoming a bridge "between the object world and the transcendent realm" (Deikman, 1982).

Reaffirmation of the Task

Viktor Frankl (1963) wrote:

> Life ultimately means taking the responsibility to find the right answer to its problems and to fulfil the tasks which it constantly sets for each individual (p. 122).

The funeral, at its conclusion, should point people to four tasks — to respond, to cope, to live and to be.

We all have a *response*. It may be automatic or impulsive, composed or troubled. We might slip into the role of long-term discontent. Or we might block off the event and its emotion, rearrange the house and get on as if nothing significant had happened. The question is: "How will we respond? What will we do now that this has happened?"

Harold Kushner (1982) made an impressive statement when he wrote:

> Is there an answer to this question of why bad things happen to good people? That depends on what we mean by "answer". If we mean — "is there an explanation which will make sense of it all?" — why is there cancer in the world? why did my father get cancer? why did the plane crash? why did my child die? — then there is probably no satisfying answer ...
>
> But the word "answer" can mean "response" as well as

"explanation", and in that sense, there may be a satisfying answer to the tragedies of our lives. The response would be Job's response in MacLeish's version of the biblical story — to forgive the world for not being perfect, to forgive God for not making a better world, to reach out to people around us, and to go on living despite it all.

In the final analysis, the question of why bad things happen to good people translates itself into some very different questions, no longer asking why something happened, but asking how we will respond, what we intend to do now that it has happened (pp. 153–4).

The second task is *to cope* with the immediate stress and the many hassles that are part of the loss and grief experience. Hitherto we have tended to admit a wide diffusion of coping as the norm for loss and grief. It is possible to say, "Apart from the meaning of the event and how I might respond, what do I have to cope with? Do I have the facilities and resources to cope?" We then remind ourselves that coping can be enhanced as we learn the skills of coping, as we sustain our self-esteem and self-efficacy and as we keep our support groups alive and functioning.

The third task is *to live* in the full context of one's identity, belonging and ideals. Though we might search frantically for someone to lean on, some teacher to give us the answer, some guru to lead us to enlightenment, we soon discover that we are all in the process of discovery. Our culture has not yet reached the stage of wisdom or eternal blessedness. We continue to "see only puzzling reflections in a mirror" (St. Paul, 1 Corinthians 13:12). But we are all participants in the process: individuals yet joined in the whole, and being so:

it allows people to be what they can be and to do what they, and only they can do ... In a Hasidic anecdote, "Before his death, Rabbi Zusya said, In the coming world, they will not ask me: Why were you not Moses? They will ask me: Why were you not Zusya?" (Deikman, 1982, p. 177).

The fourth task is *to reaffirm the fullness of being* and thus — in spite of anxiety and resistance — be, fully. Paul Tillich (1952) wrote:

> The courage to be ... unites and transcends the courage to be as a part and the courage to be as oneself. It avoids both the loss of oneself by participation and the loss of one's world by individualization. The acceptance of the God above the God of theism makes us a part of that which is not also a part, but is the ground of the whole (p. 178).

The God of theism is the God that arises out of all the attempts to conceptualize and describe what God is and how he is encountered.

Tillich said, "the ultimate source of the courage to be is the 'God above God'" (p. 176). Our fourth task is to take on this courage that arises from the God who appears when "God has disappeared in the anxiety of doubt" (p. 180), and to reaffirm the values and faith of our ultimate concern and the struggle of each human soul and the human community for a new being in face of anxiety, ambiguity and tragedy.

W. H. Auden wrote, in *Prologue at Sixty:*

> Flesh must fall through fated time
> from birth to death, both unwilled,
> but Spirit may climb counterwise
> from a death, in faith freely chosen,
> to resurrection, a re-beginning.

13

The Bonds of Love and the Ways We Love

It is loving that saves us, not loss that destroys us.

George Vaillant

*... The more I give to thee
The more I have, for both are infinite.*

Juliet in Shakespeare's *Romeo and Juliet*

*He who bends to himself a joy
Does the wingèd life destroy;
But he who kisses the Joy as it flies
lives in eternity's sunrise.*

William Blake

Love can have many meanings. It can change from relationship to relationship and it can mean different things in the same relationship at different times. Further complications occur when two people in a love relationship never actually articulate what their love is or requires; they may have never learned how to pursue the love they believe they want and, though very attached, may be wanting different things from the love they believe should be there. One may be seeking stability, warmth, support and nurture; the other may be caught up in a quest of power, excitement and self-enhancing satisfactions.

Kremen and Kremen (1971) alluded to some of the

ambiguity of the word "love" in the following way:

> You can love your grandmother, your dog, your wife of twenty years and "be in love" with your mistress all on the same day ... It pains us to accept that the ecstasy of romantic love, existing alongside its despair, may be irreconcilable with stable relationships rooted in our need for security and held together by other forces than passionate idealization (p. 139).

When couples decide to separate, they may say the love they once had has been lost. They may be still strongly attached to the person and quickly affected by their presence, their attitudes and behaviors. On the other hand they may say they no longer feel any sense of attachment or bond, but somehow they still care for and love the person. Love and attachment may persist despite anger, hostility and desperation, or the anger, hostility and desperation may be indications that the love has been eroded and the bond is being severed.

In the process of forming a bond, one person may be attracted to the other and there is an identification and sharing of interest, a divulging and exposure of the self, a growing commitment to common goals and an interweaving into each other's relationships, interests, needs, philosophies, hopes and ambitions. There is an idealization of the other, a symbolic and actual accessing and sharing of each other and a sense of being complemented and enhanced by the other. Strains come into the bond when one perceives flaws in the other, when expectations are not being fulfilled or have to be modified, and there is an experienced disjunction and confusion over what is going on or what might be going on. Love is questioned and the bond comes under threat.

Symbolic or actual withdrawal may occur. Quarrels

take place and there are expressions of anxiety, disapproval, anger and resentment. When the bond is broken the idealization, projection, accessing, complementarity and sense of completion are lost. We do notice, however, that although a couple may find they no longer love each other or demonstrate loving behavior, the bond may remain and they continue to feel attached and show various attachment behaviors. On the other hand some break the attachment but may say, "We will always love each other ... I care about her ... though we no longer are attached, I still have tender feelings." Love and attachment may persist after separation and despite anger and resentment. Others may recognize the reality of the loss and their reorganized way of living will be reflected in such words as "Yes, I loved him once, but now I see him as different, and so am I."

Some people say they find separation pains more difficult to manage than the pain of bereavement after a death. The hurt arising from these losses can take many manifestations, some of which are confusing in their apparent contradictions. A person may be very depressed or elated; they may feel an enormous burden or constriction, or a sense of liberation and relief; there may be panic, vigilance and anxiety or shallow optimism. Others may be obsessed by their search for glory with its self-idealization, the sense of being driven toward perfection, the pressures of ambition and the quest for power and prominence over others. Loss may provoke a great deal of anguish and sadness, anger and hate, the sense of being insulted, injured, treated badly and rejected. For some the separation pain may become accepted as a way of life, even evaluated as a higher way of life, and only those who have been through it could know its value and virtue. A partial truth is given an absolute and comprehensive status. A form of life in suspension, procrastination or denial may become evident, as the person avoids decisions, evades any risk, leaves the situation as it is, resists the realities and attempts to settle for a false sense of security and satisfaction.

It ought not surprise us that we have such anxiety and difficulty coping with the erosion of love and the disruption of our bonds and attachments. We are under no illusion about the life-enhancing part, and the demoralizing and distressing part, that love plays in our lives at different points of time. But from our earliest days our experiences of love and the behavior of love have been largely hit-and-miss. We have never been taught how to love. There has been the assumption that it comes naturally or that we would pick it up as we went along. It is also not surprising that people in coupled relationships surge into love and loving behavior, and when it cools off, there is little or no attempt to study the art of loving. The relationship can switch very quickly into demands and criticism, threats and abuse, withdrawal of services and satisfactions, and a reduced participation in the activities of the relationship.

Our earliest love and attachments are with our parents. Most parents now take great care with the way they love and encourage love in their children, but they are to some extent the products of the love, and damaged love, of their parents and significant people in their lives. They are also frequently struggling to sustain their own love and to control the emergence of their anger, resentment and hate. Inevitably their children become caught in some confusion.

One summer I was staying in a seaside apartment separated by a driveway from the neighboring apartment in which a man and his wife and two children (aged three and five years) were staying. Every morning about 6:30 the younger child would begin crying. This continued until about nine o'clock. At that point I felt the need to put some distance between us. If I returned at four or six o'clock, it seemed that the child had been crying all day but now the cry had reached wailing proportions. Many nights the crying could continue until nine or ten o'clock. It was usually interspersed with a complaining, threatening nasal whining of the mother and regular beltings because, as I heard the mother say, "He had to learn how to behave if people were going to look after him." To my astonishment, this behavior went on for a couple of weeks.

This was a three-year-old's perception of the world. This was his reaction to it. If he was getting much parental love I sensed he was not liking it, and yet after he received his belting I saw him walking off to the store with his mother. He was clinging to her like a prisoner of war attached to his captor. I felt he was not liking his world, and he was clearly receiving little to placate him or to help him discover that the world and its people were full of love for him. I could only suspect that unless something intervened, a boy like this would grow up with a large chip on his shoulder, suspicious and resentful, distrustful and angry. Sometimes the human psyche comes to the rescue. To help the child deal with this dreadful anxiety, repression takes over and does its work. These early experiences of love or withholding of love are thus no longer available to the memory, although they may continue to exert an influence on the person as they grow to adulthood.

The conflict is intensified as the child, in considerable and constant howling frustration or rage, hears his mother tell him and the others that she loves him. As I listened to her terrifying and revulsive shouting I thought she would probably say she really loved her child, but it became more and more evident how much she hated children and how deeply she resented her maternal experience. But again the psyche may play a further covering role. One day in the future, all these early scenes will be forgotten and the mother will be heard to say how she enjoyed these maternal years. She may even be heard to be counseling others!

Our experience of love begins in that earliest social matrix of our parents and family. The loving of our parents can be focused predominantly around their needs, values and circumstances, and the early experience of loving, and not-loving, can lead us into various anxieties and conflicts regarding our autonomy, dependence, authenticity, involvements and responsibilities. We develop many selves, many false selves, and frequently experience difficulty discriminating the real from the unreal.

We look for models upon which to base our loving. Parents are early models, sometimes of the love and behavior that we would want to follow and that would be enriching and enhancing to ourselves and others. Sometimes they are models of what we do not want. We make up our minds that we will not follow them. From time to time, however, we will be aware that we have become entangled in our own subtle and unconscious contradictions, as we discover we are imitating models that we thought we had rejected. Other models of loving are found in people we meet, in significant personages and in the characters of stories we read and the religions we follow. Some find that it is necessary or helpful to receive counseling and psychotherapy to help them get free of their attachments to some destructive or persecuting or restrictive models, and to facilitate a greater sense of autonomy and self-acceptance in developing new and more satisfying styles of loving. There is a substantial growth as we move from our symbiotic-need type of loving to a more mature awareness and experience of the varieties of loving through eros, ludus, storge, mania, pragma and agape.

Eros is the love of fascination, a powerful physical and sexual attraction and passion. *Ludus* is the enjoyment of close and loving relationships without involvement and specific commitment. *Storge* is the slow-burning, evolving type of love. *Mania* is a possessive, demanding, jealous, consuming love without self-confidence and stable control or judgment. *Pragma* is the calculating rational love that looks at benefits and deficits and pragmatically makes its choices. *Agape* is the love of compassion, charity and caring.

Much of our early love in a couple relationship is strongly of the eros and mania types. We may move to storge and pragma, and come to express our love through compassion, charity and care. When a couple relationship is strained, or expectations are not being fulfilled, one or both partners may convert their love into compassionate action toward other people or within particular organizations to which they belong.

Love does not readily retire. After loss and pain it seems to return and places before us the choice of staying in isolated anguish or following its invitation once again, whether into a new relationship or into caring action. Some believe and confirm for themselves that once love has been lost, it can never be found again.

One husband, who had been married for twenty-seven years, found the death of his wife difficult to accommodate. "We were always together," he said, "We were the epitome of John Donne's poem."

No man is an Island, entire of itself; every man is a piece of
the Continent, a part of the main.

He had limited the cosmic dimensions of Donne's
poem to apply it to his marital relationship and thus at
his wife's death he went on to say, "When she died, something in me died. I could never love anyone again."

Some live out such self-made or self-attributed
prophecy. They build walls around themselves, withhold
themselves, become hardened and resentful, stoic or
ethereal. They adopt behaviors and attitudes that ensure
a sustained distance or a controlled interaction. They set
themselves on a pathetic course of the half-lived life. It
is pathetic because it is an unnecessary state that is self-
imposed (and sometimes endorsed by family and society).
I have seen many people who have been believing and
living out this kind of misappropriated loyalty and destiny
discover with some astonishment that their responsibility
to life was not inevitably and irrevocably dependent on
the life and death of their spouse.

We do not underestimate the significance of a love one
partner can develop and sustain for the other, or the
strong bonds of loyalty, mutual dependence and care, and
the shared good-fun that are the valued ingredients of a
friendly life-enhancing relationship. There is, however,
another reality — that many couples do not have this
kind of relationship. It may be a love of external appearance, pretense and shallowness, and a refusal to accept or
acknowledge that given a better chance they would
choose a relationship different from this and would put
high on their priorities ingredients noticeably absent from
their current relationship. Some are caught up more with
the bond than with the love; others sustain a kind of love

to fill the empty spaces and to avoid the anxiety of ever facing the implications of those spaces.

There is the love of interpersonal contact — the expectation of this love is that "he" will be there: "It would be lonely without him." There is a level of interpersonal acceptance and tolerance: "Nobody else would put up with him." And his reciprocation: "I don't know what I'd do without her." Various needs and services are supplied and many do what is necessary to sustain the semblance of love in order to sustain the services and avoid the anxiety of any disturbance. Although there is a degree of experienced and expressed mutuality, individuals within such a relationship work quickly to find a replacement when one is lost.

Much of our loving is woven into a fantasy. Though our current relationship may be banal, we may keep alive the wish and the fantasy of one day finding what we always hoped to find. That does not always happen, and we are required then to find ways to cope with that disappointment and unfulfilled aspect of life. Sometimes the fantasy finds its reality.

Bertrand Russell (1967) was one who found that the fantasy and wish could be fulfilled. In his late seventies he wrote:

> Three passions, simple but overwhelmingly strong, have governed my life: the longing for love, the search for knowledge, and unbearable pity for the suffering of mankind. These passions, like great winds, have blown me hither and thither, in a wayward course, over a deep ocean of anguish, reaching to the very verge of despair.
>
> I have sought love, first, because it brings ecstasy — ecstasy so great that I would often have sacrificed all the rest of my life for a few hours of this joy. I have sought it next, because it relieves loneliness — that terrible loneliness in

which one shivering consciousness looks over the rim of the world into the cold fathomless lifeless abyss. I have sought it, finally, because in the union of love I have seen, in a mystic miniature, the prefiguring vision of the heaven that saints and poets have imagined. This is what I have sought, and though it might seem too good for human life, this is what — at last — I have found.

The fantasy component can sometimes take a different expression. A person may feel bound and tied to another person but it is a fantasy bond that is being sustained. This is experienced first in childhood when the child feels that the relationship he thought he had with his parent is in conflict or suffers some hurt. The child clings to the illusion of that strong connection, but ultimately it is a fantasy which becomes a defense protecting the child against further emotional anxiety and pain. In adult life, this process continues as the person attempts to find a parent in other persons or institutions or in themselves. Apart from how this bond might be established in childhood, we see in adults a partnership that keeps the forms of love but is a fantasy of love. This fantasy is maintained long after they have stopped behaving in a loving manner. They usually remain together more out of addiction and perceived external constraints than out of a genuine desire.

Robert Firestone (1985) wrote:

Without realizing it, most people become deadened to their emotions. Early in their lives they turn their backs on themselves, their real desires and wants, and substitute self-nourishing habits and fantasies that only serve to deaden them. They have ceased to want what they say they want because real gratifications and accomplishments threaten the process of self-nourishment through fantasy (p. 28).

Many of our loves thus fulfill needs and purposes that are not always recognized. A love or a bond can be a mediation-line to something else. One partner may use the relationship as part of their success, status, identity and security. There may be no love or loving behavior within the relationship, but these other objectives and needs become paramount, and sometimes become obsessions. In the longer term, a couple may bask in their achievement of having had a long partnership but never acknowledge what kept the partnership in place. There is a denial of how much the other partner was involved in a mediation-line, a means to an end.

When we find ourselves capable of being involved in different kinds of love and loving behavior, it should not be surprising that when a love is lost or impaired, the effects on the people concerned vary widely. In the one person, the pain of loss relating to two loved people will take a different form. We see this in the case of Lawrie, aged 38.

He was a father of two girls aged 11 and 14 years, and a boy aged 8. The boy fell from his bicycle on a busy road, was struck by a car and killed. Lawrie found his grief reactions extremely difficult. His wife recovered and took all the action necessary to reorganize the home after the boy's death, but Lawrie could not face any of these tasks. When the boy's name was mentioned he would withdraw, struggling to evade another bout of tears and grieving.

A year after the boy was killed Lawrie's father, aged 71, died. One Sunday afternoon he was sitting on his veranda reading a book. When his wife called him for the evening meal she discovered him dead. Lawrie was his only son; there were four daughters born before him. His father was very determined to have a son and Lawrie was the fifth and necessary final attempt to achieve this goal. There had always been a strong bond of love and admiration between them, which had increased and matured over the years. Why then was Lawrie able to take over every detail of his father's funeral and proudly speak to every relative and friend about his father, whereas he was incapable of handling any matter regarding his son?

He said he loved his father as much as he loved his son, but "it was different." As Lawrie explained: "With my father, it seemed our love had had the time to settle; with my son, there was so much unfinished business both ways. We were still a father and son rather than two people. Strangely, you do what a father should do and what a son inevitably does. You know you love them, but somehow you don't really get that in place. You are always involved in doing and demanding, rather than allowing things to happen as they should. Then when you suddenly find you have lost them, you realize you were preoccupied with the wrong things. You feel guilt and shame and terrible frustration and helplessness. At first you want to fight the helplessness but it wins every time."

With Lawrie we see that the love he had for his father enabled him to separate from his father and let him go, enriched by the overall relationship. But the love he had for his son was still caught up in external activities, and the separation was a terrifying thought with invasions of guilt, shame, anger and helplessness. Separation from the father was an enabling experience; separation from the son was threatening to his future adaptation and enjoyment, and made him prone to recurring death wishes and self-destructive behavior. In Lawrie's relationship with his father, love and gratitude had joined together. In his relationship with his son, love and hope were still joined. Hope is always endangered, always vulnerable, and when it is shattered the reactions can be varied and diffuse.

Lawrie was still entangled in the desire to hold onto his son and to some extent restricted the son's separation and individuation. In effect he was still conflicted about his son's own self-identity and he was still doing "external activities" to establish that identity. To some extent he may have been using his son to hold onto his own "inner child": the son was the symbol of his own continuing fantasy, all of which was ruptured with the death of the son. When his son died Lawrie found he was no longer loving but hating — hating life, hating death, hating himself, hating others, even hating a part of the son that allowed himself to be killed. The father split off the love he had for the son and increasingly had access only to the hate. He grieved and told himself he did not love the boy, did not love him enough or properly. He wanted to "steel himself" against love and tenderness, but whenever it was mentioned he was unable to cope with it.

He became so preoccupied with his grief and self-distress and self-hate that he could not remember what he loved; nor did he allow that love to do its work. He became preoccupied with the loss as a disruption — which it was — but overlooked how his love was enabling the son to separate and individuate just as he had done with his father, and as he himself ultimately would have done with his son. We sometimes overlook that just as the son must mature and individuate from his parents, so the parents must mature, separate and individuate from their son.

Lawrie had had time to stabilize internally his relationship with his father, but did not have time to do the same with his son. Where a relationship is unsettled or is in conflict, internally, it is more difficult to let it go. Similarly if the person never did establish an individuality of his own then, not surprisingly, when the person on whom he is dependent dies, he feels as if part of him has died also.

Persistent recall of memories and events, repetitive visits to the cemetery or crematorium, can reflect a preoccupation with the person who has died and an anxiety over a part of the self which is perceived to be shattered or lost. What is required is an internal reassessment of the love that existed, and with the self reorganized, the person is strengthened to develop a new life-style.

There are people who claim they have been so hurt and injured by love and its loss that they will never be the same. We know that loss, separation and tragedy are part of the human story, but when they happen to us we find them very difficult to accept. We tend to blame our unsettled and traumatized state on the loss, the unfairness and cruelty of life or the withdrawal of God's love. Albert Einstein once said, "God does not play dice," but sometimes our experience tempts us to believe he does!

The hurt that is suffered may not be due to the loss or to the disruption of the bonds of attachment, per se. Other factors may be involved: people may not know how to sustain vitality and spontaneity or how to give timbre and color to their communications. They may not know how to change a relationship, how to terminate it and separate without destructiveness. They may have never learned effective means of coping with the hurt of love, and therefore will act to deny the hurt, avoid dealing with it, distort it or allow it to blow out into other areas of the relationship and other facets of life.

The kind of hurt suffered will depend on the perception and experience of the relationship before the loss occurred — on the personality of the person, the management of earlier experiences of loss, the capacities of resilience, flexibility and hardiness. Personal resources like self-esteem and self-worth, optimism, expectancy, a philosophy of life and the way events are interpreted and integrated into experience will be important. Interested audiences, and audiences perceived to be interested, will affect a person's reactions, as will the degree to which that person sees there is a supportive environment and that alternative solutions are possible and acceptable.

This book has put forward a different conception of intervention in the hurts of life. It has also described coping strategies and resources. As these are accepted and put into action they will play an important part in limiting the hurt that people suffer, and in the more effective management of those hurts.

Throughout this book we have seen how people will blame others for the trauma, for their reaction and for the protraction of that reaction; for their own heightened emotionality and vulnerability and the behavior and health of their children. Though we would like to believe that people would want to get over their hurts, to get over the pains and the disappointments of love, we find that many factors collude to prolong the state of distress and exacerbate it. We would expect people to seek the relief of pain and the goals of happiness, pleasure and the joy of life, but they frequently do not, and claim that it is not right that they should.

We have seen that the healing process is inhibited by the dogmas and dicta that people and their communities adopt regarding loss, death and grief. There are misunderstandings, a lack of information and a very low level of awareness regarding the possibilities. People have tended to flounder on blindly and sometimes their helpers have accepted that floundering as part of the healing process rather than as an indication of a need for some help to get out of their confused state of helplessness.

Many are not only impeded by their information and lack of it, they are understandably unprepared for the traumas that confront them. I frequently see a parent who does not know how to anchor the emotional reactions of the children as they try to accept the loss of the other parent. They have no models, very little helpful information, and in the turmoil of it all, they are often unable to organize their own experiences and accumulated wisdom to focus constructively on the rapidly changing situation. The whole experience can become like a nightmare which itself tends to provoke further cycles of instability and turbulence. Alongside such experiences, it is important to note others — there are people who say that they have never had to deal with a crisis before, that they have always thought of themselves as ineffective and inadequate, but when confronted by a specific crisis, they coped and were major resources for others in their coping. Thus although we look for the way people have handled earlier stresses, and the way they have organized their own strengths and personality resources through their lives, these factors obviously do not in themselves determine the outcome.

A particular trauma can trigger a transitory chaos or a more prolonged distress or a neurosis that may have been dormant to this point in time. We have seen how people have endured outrageous brutality and multiple losses and have regained their capacity to live happily, appreciatively and generously — until one apparently minor event occurs, to be the trigger for a long depression. They may say, "I have finally reached the conclusion that God is punishing me for something." Others find that an event can trigger a great deal of self-punishment, a sense of failure and self-denigration. At times it appears they have joined forces with some punitive inner parent; at other times it is as if the good parent has never been there, or cannot be found, and a primitive punitive destructiveness runs out of control.

Loss of love can trigger an anxiety of doubt regarding self-worth, loneliness and the person's capacity to cope on their own. In some circumstances the dependence that has become part of the relationship over its history has meant that the sense of autonomy has been played down and self-resources have not been developed. With the loss of the relationship the immediacy of that dependence can bring back memories and fears of earlier experiences of helplessness, rejection and inadequacy. It can also provide a wide range of irrational demands of what people "should" and "should not" do, and what the hurt person "must" have in order to be happy again. This state of helplessness and hurt can be so persuasive that people believe no solution will ever be found, that no effort will make any difference. But along with this is the paradox — "Surely someone can help me" — and a continuing expectation that people will help. This attitude, and the mode of being which it becomes, are often confirmed by people in the environment who, in being too persistently helpful, do not challenge the hurting person to confront their new reality and their own resources. Just as some infants are content to be placid and good so long as they are well-fed, so adults promulgate this oral dependence into the way they react to the frustrations and traumas of their lives. This becomes a tenacious and resistant impediment to the healing process.

We would all stand to cope better with the crises of life and the erosion and loss of our bonds and attachments if we were better prepared. For the most part, despite a large body of knowledge gathered from the last fifty years of psychological research and clinical practice, we do little organized thinking and preparation for those known and necessary losses and even less for the unexpected and imposed losses. Some experiences are now readily identifiable as constructive factors for preparation and prevention.

We now recognize the value of experiences and environments that inculcate and strengthen self-esteem, self-efficacy, autonomy and resilience. There are the coping strategies, many of which have been set out in different sections of this book. According to coping psychology, our inner wounds, our symptoms of distress and the physiological and relationship disturbances are outcomes of a mismatch between the demands that people perceive are being made upon them, and their capacities, and perceived capacities, to cope with those demands. When a person has adequate coping skills and strategies they are more able to intercept an emerging problem, control its impact on their lives and prevent it from becoming a hazard to their health, or a recurring threat to their sense of well-being. This notion persistently presents an optimistic view of the human being and an active responsive view of the part people can play in managing the problems and pains of their life.

Support groups, and the nature and content of human environments, are important influences in preparing people for their crises and helping them cope with them. Some groups and environments, while ostensibly offering sympathetic help and information, tend to prolong grief and suffering virtually as a way of honoring what has been lost. These experiences can trigger a range of unhelpful ruminations as well as a general evasion of adapting to the new reality. Support groups, acting effectively, can alter the person's perception of the crisis and of the resources available to them. They help sustain self-confidence, coping strategies and a positive view of the future, and become a direct influence on the person's happiness, health and sense of well-being (Macnab, 1984).

An attitude and philosophy of life can have a transforming influence on a tragic event so that it becomes a life-enhancing experience. Some forms of loving which are strong and genuine, when lost, are viewed as sources of satisfaction and inspiration. The surviving person expresses gratitude, expansiveness, an awe for having been in a love relationship with the person who has died. They have been able to absorb and organize the deficits, conflicts and hostilities, and to give them perspective in the greater comprehension of their relationship. The relationship and the loss have been internalized and organized in such a way as to evoke a sustained and settled response.

"It was a great experience ... an experience that nobody would like to miss or lose ... but I had it ... and I'm grateful beyond words that I had it ... now it has gone. I could spend years lamenting that it has gone. But its impact would then be a burden instead of an inspiration. I want the whole experience to be part of my next phase of life in the sense that it was a marvelous experience to be together for that short time in the whole of eternity when we were able to chip into the mountain face the footholds for either one of us to climb up further."

Thus the loss of the person has a positive significance for the survivor and for others around the survivor who may become a valued model and inspiration. It becomes an important factor in the environment and social matrix in which the person continues to live.

Marjorie Pizer's poem *The Existence of Love* focuses on the awareness that a relationship is a gift. The loss of the gift inevitably leads us to mourn the loss until once more we see the significance of the gift in the context of onward growing:

I had thought that your death
Was a waste and a destruction,
A pain of grief hardly to be endured.
I am only beginning to learn
that your life was a gift and a growing
And a loving left with me.
The desperation of death
destroyed the existence of love,
But the fact of death
Cannot destroy what has been given.
I am learning to look at your life again
Instead of your death and your departing.

Music, literature, meditation, nature and fantasy can bring their healing and restorative influences. Another poem, *My Healing*, by Marjorie Pizer speaks of the healing warmth of the sun:

I sat in my desolation
Withdrawn from all around,
Feeling my life was a ruin, a failure.
I was empty inside
With the utter collapse of my being.
I did not care any more
For living or dying.
I was alone
In my distress and desolation.
But as I sat sadly on the ground,
The sun reached out his hand to me
And touched my face
And so my healing began.

Psychoanalyst Harold F. Searles (1985) recalled one of his favorite fairy tales, which he used to read to his children. It concerned a beloved Grandpa Bunny who, upon his death, turned into a beautiful sunset. The story engenders a joyful process of life and death linked with the cycles of nature; it holds a view of death, and a buoyant hope about the dead loved one, that is positive and powerfully regenerative.

Imagery, both in itself and as it is involved in a systematic and planned way in psychotherapy, plays a more important part in healing the wounds of the mind and drawing us into the future than most people realize. The imagery of Olive Schreiner's story (Luthman, 1982) links the individual's apprehension with a much wider context, and in doing so conveys a strong sense of hope in spite of loss:

"For what do I go to this far land which no one has ever reached? Oh, I am alone! I am utterly alone!"

And Reason, that old man, said to her, "Silence! What do you hear?"

And she listened intently, and she said, "I hear a sound of feet, a thousand times ten thousand and thousand of thousands, and they beat this way!"

He said, "They are the feet of those that shall follow you. Lead on! Make a track to the water's edge! Where you stand now, the ground will be beaten flat by ten thousand times ten thousand feet."

And he said, "Have you seen the locusts how they cross a stream? First one comes down to the water-edge, and is swept away, and then another comes and then another, and then another, and at last with their bodies piled up a bridge is built and the rest pass over."

She said, "And, of those that come first, some are swept away and are heard of no more; their bodies do not even build the bridge?"

"And are swept away, and are heard of no more — and what of that?" he said.

"And what of that—" she said.

"They make a track to the water's edge."

"They make a track to the water's edge!"

And she said, "Over that bridge which shall be built with our bodies, who will pass?"

He said, "The entire human race."

And the woman grasped her staff.

And I saw her turn down that dark path to the river (p. 14f).

Dante, facing the prospect of journeying through a terrible hell, was met by Virgil, who had been sent to be his companion and guide. Virgil reassured Dante:

"Wherefore, I judge this fittest in thy case
That I should lead thee, and thou follow in faith,
To journey hence through an eternal place,
Where thou shalt hear cries of despairing breath,
Shalt look on the ancient spirits in their pain,
Such that each calls out for a second death."

Dante answered:

"Lead me where thou hast spoken of but now,
so that my eyes St Peter's gate may find.
And those whom thou portrayest in such woe!"
Then he moved onward: and I went behind.

Religious imagery, beliefs and practices, and a religious world-view, provide many people with a way of coping and a way of understanding themselves, their crises and their adaptation to the realities of life. Probably most people have some, albeit inarticulate, apprehension of "something beyond them," which they might call "God," or "the fellow upstairs." Others may use the images of God as a person, heaven as a place and angels as actual helpers. Some say, "Our father is safe in heaven; he is better off there." A gravestone in a cemetery carried the inscription "God needed another angel."

Many people would find these words, and the assurance they imply, unsatisfying. They do not look for a three-tiered view of the universe (heaven–earth–hell) nor for the literalist images of angels. But they do earnestly search for some view of healing in times of loss and death, and to be part of what J. D. Sutherland (1983) called "the great human expressive needs." Religion has often been seen as man's weakness, promulgating his dependency and fear, and an infantile apprehension of a God who is too like a conflicted parent in his pleasure-giving and punitive actions.

Another view of religion sees life as the highest and most sacred cause. It is given to us all. It is not so much a right that we all have, but a sharing in an extraordinary expression of mystery and grace: that we are part of life and can make some contribution to it. It is open for us to soak it up selfishly, to be apathetic or resentful, or to explore its potential, its expressiveness and its fullness. Everybody who has life is bound into it. The word "religion" means to be bound into something: we are bound into life, and since we say the Source and Fullness of life is God, in a manner of speaking, we are bound into God.

That binding is also a freedom — for we are free to make nothing of life, or everything of it! As we explore our highest potential, we find that it is necessarily actualized in the social and interpersonal context — in the I–Thou relationship, where genuine dialogue, coexistence, expectancy and love are the highest expressions of hope and human behavior.

The way of loving therefore becomes both an act of grace and a task of our responsiveness. We emerge from the pain of our losses to convert our lost love into a new love of compassion and care.

14

A Better Management

Let your life lightly dance on the edges of time like dew on the tip of a leaf.

Rabindranath Tagore

What does achieving recovery mean? It means once again being able to do some perfectly ordinary things. Being able to feel good if something good happens. Being able to be hopeful about the future. Being able to give attention to everyday life. Being able to be cheerful. Being able to feel at peace with yourself.

Robert S. Weiss

Throughout this discussion on loss and grief I have put forward the view that grief and mourning can be greatly assisted and accelerated by applying contemporary psychotherapeutic knowledge and practice to these difficult expressions of human pain. We know that one experience of loss differs from another; that some people's resources, knowledge, adaptability and resilience will differ from others'. We recognize that the objective circumstances of the loss will inevitably affect people in different ways, will affect adults differently from children, and that reactions will be reprovoked under differing actual, and symbolic, circumstances.

The long-awaited death of a 93-year-old man will be perceived as expected and appropriate, even as overdue. But the murder of a six-year-old girl by a psychotic father will be perceived as tragic and will evoke distressing reactions in a wide range of people. In times when technology and communication systems bring deaths from war and genocide and various natural catastrophes right into our living rooms, our reactions to these recurring mega-deaths, as well as to our own intimate family deaths, inevitably become confused. On the one hand there is a tendency to become case-hardened, protected from reality by the screens of technology and of our own psychic desensitization. On the other hand we are struck by the utter horror of it and by the sheer human impotence in the face of overwhelming forces. In the instances of kidnap, torture and death by the powers of the State, families of victims are left in a particularly helpless and disturbed state. They know their loved one could be dead, but they refuse to admit it. Unable to see for themselves, and without any information, they become convinced that the person must be dead. But this conviction becomes loaded with guilt, as unconsciously it becomes interwoven with the death wish, and when the news of the death is ultimately confirmed, they fear they may have been the cause of it.

Images play a powerful — even obsessive — part in people's attempts to make sense of their situation. They are likely to become preoccupied with images of how the person died, their last hours and their last thoughts. These images tend to block out other memories, and virtually force the mourner to see each day's experiences through the peculiar tunnel vision of these images. It is not surprising that people with such constant preoccupations hear voices, catch fleeting glimpses of the dead person, indulge in magical thinking and various forms of idealization of the dead person.

This strongly emphasizes the need for grief workers to be skilled in methods of helping people reconstruct their inner thoughts and imagery. This applies with more conviction to helping children entangled in their grief. Children generally do not have a body of experience behind them, they have not had the time to develop attitudes and belief systems, and their inner psychic stability is unstructured. Without careful support, the minds of children can "run riot" as they imagine all possibilities, see ghosts, make up stories and work out their own ways to settle in their minds something that resists settlement.

With both children and adults, some later event or crisis, some symbolic happening, some discussion or thought, may reactivate distress and mourning. Being aware of this possibility, we can take steps to help them expect it, and deal with it as it occurs. Without this preparation and learning, the mourners begin to accept the belief that they will never get over it, or that they cannot cope, will not be worthy of another relationship, or that they are going mad. The conventional mourning practices do not take adequate cognizance of the repetitive aspects of a person's disorganization and helplessness. The more specific and systematic management of grief reactions will certainly do so.

In recent times, the emergence of AIDS has added a further complexity to grief and mourning. Society generally has had difficulty accepting the realities of this disease and has initially recoiled with a horror that engendered ideas of the "destruction of everybody." Families most affected have been deeply confused in their reactions, simultaneously loving and hating, moved by compassion and outraged by the fear and stigma. The companions of the dying one have wanted to accept fully what was occurring, but have also acted in ways to deny it. We see in the AIDS situation, as clearly as in other grief situations, the need to distinguish between what is occurring and people's reactions to what is occurring. When people are able to recognize the reality of the situation and of their own reactions they begin to be in a position to choose and change. Repetitive talking over the situation, or expressing feelings or over-preoccupation with the dying or dead one, will be no substitute for the systematic deliberate work involved in discovering and developing new ways of thinking and reorganizing and settling the ruminations of the mind. AIDS victims know — probably more than many — the part that fear can play in people's lives. We cannot get rid of fear completely but we can develop rational ways to manage it and limit its effects.

In all management of grief, if people do not take the risk of moving beyond the self-constructed safety zones that seem to offer some sanctuary from fear, then the fear remains and their response to life is thus impaired.

Loss and grief, no matter by what event or experience they come to the human individual or the human community, are difficult and complex stresses. They can sweep individuals and communities into complex pain: physical, mental and spiritual pain. If people have no developed capacity to intercept the ongoing effects of loss and grief, these effects can disrupt morale and health, love and work, self-esteem and autonomy, the sense of being a functional and coping person, the enjoyable interaction in relationships and the capacity to make a stimulating contribution to the human environment.

Everyone is affected by their losses. Everyone experiences grief. While in the past we have taken an individualistic and limited approach to grief, we are recognizing more clearly now that losses and their management can affect an individual's happiness and well-being in the short term, but that they also affect their attitude and role in the world for their whole lifetime. A relocation of home, migration to another country, divorce, death, a funeral — all are regarded as everyday events. People are thought to make their adjustments and get on with living.

That is far from reality. And the costs of the reality are enormous. Family life, emotional and psychological health and physical well-being may be affected. There is also the vast economic loss that occurs through demoralization and depression, unresolved problems, and the lack of effective education and support groups to help people move methodically through their loss and grief reactions.

Much of the pain and anguish of loss and grief could be prevented. Few are interested in prevention. Perhaps there is the belief that "We are doing all right" or "We'll deal with it when it happens" or "It's not such a big deal." Denial also plays some part, as does the communal accommodation to the daily television screening of death scenes without any follow-through to the traumatic disorganization and pain those deaths bring to the next of kin and communities.

There is a widely held view that if and when some loss or grief occurs, someone will be there to help. That is usually how it is — each instance receives some help — but the human race is hardly enhanced, and generationally we make little or no progress in managing a problem that affects all mankind.

Our better management of loss and grief will depend a great deal on adults learning from didactic and experiential situations how they form attachments and how they sever them, and how they can apply therapeutic experience and wisdom to deal specifically with their aches and pains and their consequential reactions. Adults will take this learning to their children. This whole educational process requires a status and priority that it has never been given before. Our community's sharpening focus on the meaning of health and wholeness, the fully functioning human being, and the aspirations of living the most effective stimulating life possible, will help bring this educational process more into public notice and demand.

The process will necessarily be hindered so long as we do not have professionals trained to carry out these programs. In the diverse field of training therapists and counselors from many disciplines, very little time is given to the psychotherapies that are relevant to loss and grief. It is common to find analysts, therapists and counselors with training in the therapeutics for some of the most exotic conditions (which may be rarely encountered) but with no training whatever in the appropriate therapeutics for the most common traumas associated with loss and grief. The growth of the group calling themselves grief counselors could help change this situation in our community. It may also bring some change in the training of other therapists and counselors. But the grief counselors too will need to make a mind-shift away from some preoccupation with the body, with catharsis and the accepted grief work, in order to adopt and learn the ways set out in this book that will lead to a more systematic management of these many and diverse problems.

An educational process on its own will fail. This vast human and communal need requires that the educational process be integrated with the establishment of supervised support groups. These groups will be made up of people who will have been in a learning group themselves to develop an awareness of the role support people can play for specific problems. Some people will discover that they have greater empathy for people who have no brothers or sisters and who have lost a parent; others might feel drawn to a support group for those grieving for a person who died of a specific illness or disease. All support groups require an ongoing training program. They all require regular supervisory contact with a professional leader skilled in the special area of our concern of loss and grief. We have witnessed several grief support groups develop, having the highest and best intentions, but without adequate training and ongoing supervision. Some of these groups have become ideologically and emotionally committed to particular views and practices, with dogmas, and impedences to growth, never far away.

As we recognize the implications of the management of loss and grief for the whole of society, we need to look more critically at the funeral industry. In the last decade there has been a significant revolution among the funeral directors, as they have reviewed their role, clarified their objectives, provided training and support for their staff and developed grief counseling seminars for the community, the churches and professional helpers. These developments are both timely and commendable. Funeral directors and the industry generally are to be encouraged to proceed further in educating the community to a more rational management of the funeral, and this will mean taking a more leading role in breaking with customs that hold people in their grief.

The funeral industry would expect me to raise that common and well-known sensitivity of their cost and the profits that are involved. In times when phobias regarding taxation abound, it is unlikely that any government would want to take over this industry. But it does involve a basic community and social service. The industry itself is aware that there are companies practicing within it that do not place a high priority on ethical standards. There is also room for reviewing the profit motive of the industry. It is an industry that has taken an impressive leap forward in its maturity and it would seem that it could now look toward a nonprofit status without losing its high regard for community service.

Doctors and clergy have an important role to play, especially in the experiences of relocation, separation, divorce and bereavement, and with the new life-styles they will bring. Within the body of this book, I have set out ways whereby the funeral can be restructured. But doctors and clergy have an ongoing function in helping the community reach out to better ways of grieving and more mature attitudes and management of death. They could also help in establishing support groups.

These roles and tasks are so important and necessary that they should not be left to occur only where local interest or initiatives seem to be present. They are of such priority concern for health and well-being, adaptation and productivity, that doctors and clergy should have a leadership and regular involvement in them. The basic and ongoing training of doctors and clergy ought to include specific courses and programs on managing the various situations of loss and grief, and in that process, what this book proposes will be a helpful ingredient.

Our overall concern, as expressed here, is that we move beyond a generalized grieving process which can have extensive and disturbing implications and consequences for individuals, families and society, to a more informed management of loss and grief that focuses on specific needs and situations. Our overall objective is to relieve human suffering, anguish and pain — strategically — as soon as possible. We aim to help individuals and their communities to shape their attitudes, behaviors and life-styles, to uncover their strengths and resilience, and bring them back into the mainstream of life again with their health and well-being and view of the world protected and, wherever possible, enhanced.

Bibliography

Bonime, W. "Anxiety: Feared Loss of Functional Effectiveness," *Contemporary Psychoanalysis*, 1981, 17, 1, pp. 69–90.

Cairns, D. *An Autobiography*, S.C.M.: London, 1950.

Capra, F. "Holistic Health — Holistic Peace," in Bliss, S. (ed.), *The New Holistic Health Handbook*, Stephen Greenes Press: Lexington, Mass., 1985.

Dante, A. *The Divine Comedy*, Penguin: Harmondsworth, England, 1982.

Deikman, A.J. *The Observing Self: Mysticism and Psychotherapy*, Beacon Press: Boston, 1982.

Firestone, R.W. *The Fantasy Bond — Structure of Psychological Defenses*, Human Sciences Press: New York, 1985.

Ford, C.V. *The Somatizing Disorders*, Elsevier Science Publishing: New York, 1983.

Frankl, V. *Man's Search for Meaning*, Washington Square Press: New York, 1963.

Freud, S. "Mourning and Melancholia" (1917) in *Collected Papers*, Vol. IV, Hogarth: London, 1940.

Furman, E. *A Child's Parent Dies*, Yale University Press: New Haven, Conn., 1974.

Horney, K. *Neurosis and Human Growth*, Norton: New York, 1950.

James, W. *The Varieties of Religious Experience: A Study in Human Nature*, Longmans, Green: London, 1902.

Kaufmann, W. *Without Guilt and Justice*, Peter H. Wyden: New York, 1973.

Kazantzakis, N. *The Fratricides,* Bruno Cassirer: Oxford, 1963.

Knight, M. *William James,* Penguin: Harmondsworth, England, 1950.

Kremen, H. and Kremen, B. "Romantic Love and Idealization," *American Journal of Psychoanalysis,* 1971, 31, 2, pp. 134–43.

Kushner, H.S. *When Bad Things Happen To Good People,* Pan: London, 1982.

Laing, R.D. *Wisdom, Madness, & Folly,* Macmillan: London, 1985.

Lankton, S.R. and Lankton, C.H. *The Answer Within: A Clinical Framework of Ericksonian Hypnotherapy,* Brunner/Mazel: New York, 1983.

Levenson, E.A. "A Perspective on Responsibility," *Contemporary Psychoanalysis,* 1978, 14, 4, pp. 571–8.

Lifton, R.J. "The Sense of Immortality: On Death and the Continuity of Life," *American Journal of Psychoanalysis,* 1973, 33, 1, pp. 3–15.

Luthman, S.G. *Energy and Personal Power,* Mehetabel: San Rafael, Calif., 1982.

MacLaine, S. *Dancing in the Light,* Bantam Books: New York, 1985.

Macnab, F.A. *Conflict and Stress, The Malcolm Millar Lecture in Psychotherapy* (1983), Aberdeen University Press: Aberdeen, Scotland, 1984.

Macnab, F.A. *Coping,* Hill of Content: Melbourne, 1985.

Marcus, H. and Nurius, P. "Possible Selves," *American Psychologist,* 1986, 41, 9, pp. 954–69.

Russell, B. *Autobiography of Bertrand Russell,* Allen and Unwin: London and Boston, 1967.

Sales, E. *et al.*, "Victim Readjustment Following Assault," *Journal of Social Issues*, 1984, 40, 1, pp. 117–36.

Searles, H.F. "Separation and Loss in Borderline Patients," *American Journal of Psychoanalysis*, 1985, 45, 1, pp. 9–27.

Seligman, M.E.P. *Helplessness*, Freeman: San Francisco, 1975.

Sutherland, J.D. "The Self and Object Relations: A Challenge to Psychoanalysis," *Bulletin of the Menninger Clinic*, 1983, 47, 6, pp. 525–54.

Tillich, P. *The Courage To Be*, Nisbet: London, 1952.

Tillich, P. *Systematic Theology*, Vol. 1, Nisbet: London, 1953.

Tillich, P. *Systematic Theology*, Vol. 3, Nisbet: London, 1964.

Wallerstein, J.S. "Children of Divorce: The Psychological Tasks of the Child," *American Journal of Orthopsychiatry*, 1983, 53, 2, pp. 230–43.

Wilber, K. *No Boundary*, New Science Library, Shambhala: Boston and London, 1979.